# Preaching
## about
# People

# Preaching
### about
# People

## The *POWER of BIOGRAPHY*

## J. Ellsworth Kalas

CHALICE
PRESS
ST. LOUIS, MISSOURI

Biblical quotations, unless otherwise noted, are from the *New Revised Standard Version Bible*, copyright 1989, Division of Christian Education of the National Council of the Churches of Christ in the United States of America. Used by permission. All rights reserved.

Cover and interior design: Elizabeth Wright

This book is printed on acid-free, recycled paper.

Visit Chalice Press on the World Wide Web at
www.chalicepress.com

10  9  8  7  6  5  4  3  2  1          05  06  07  08  09

**Library of Congress Cataloging–in–Publication Data**

Kalas, J. Ellsworth, 1923-
  Preaching about people : the power of biography / J. Ellsworth Kalas.
    p. cm.
  ISBN-13: 978-0-827230-02-8 (pbk. : alk. paper)
  ISBN-10: 0-827230-02-8
  1. Biographical preaching.  I. Title.
  BV4235.B56K35 2004
  251–dc22
                                                    2004011569

# Contents

# Introduction
## *Stories That Should Be Told*

The week-by-week preacher must constantly be on the lookout for new homiletical possibilities. Sundays come around at an astonishing speed, often in advance of the insights that are supposed to accompany them. We'd like for our congregations to sit up straight as the sermon begins, to be lifted by the excitement of their expectancy, but it's hard to hope for such expectancy from the congregation if there's a sense of same-old-thing in the heart of the preacher.

### Searching for Variety

I am an almost fanatical believer in the continuing newness and excitement of the scriptures. Nevertheless we preachers are a human lot, and we need variety to stimulate our thinking.That means we need to find variety that has enough content and character to stir our creativity without sacrificing depth and integrity. As for the people to whom we preach, many of them hear us with the prejudice that neither we nor the scriptures live in their world. Anything we can do to counter that prejudice is gain.

The need for variety is all the greater for the preacher who also has a Sunday evening service and/or a continuing midweek event. Special banquets and celebrations come our way, when some well-meaning program chair says, "Could you give just a little talk? It wouldn't have to be a real sermon. Maybe just twenty minutes or so?"

With all this in mind, I recommend using an occasional biographical sermon. I'm not speaking of the traditional biographical

1

sermon drawn from biblical characters; I'm speaking of sermons built around the life and thinking of some person of post-biblical times. In most cases this person will probably be well known; though in our historically-challenged age, it's increasingly difficult to find such persons. On the other hand, the person may be known only to those with some specialized interest. In that case the impact will be particularly great for those who have such an interest, but we will have to work harder to gain the interest of others. We might even choose an individual who is unfamiliar to everyone in the congregation, particularly if it is one of those persons whose impact is still being felt by millions of people, even though the person's name is now largely forgotten.

This kind of preaching is not every-Sunday fare. For the major worship hour on Sunday, probably two or three times a year is often enough. The impact of these occasions can be out of proportion to their frequency, especially in their appeal to lay persons of specialized interests. Also, the incidental benefit to the preacher's creativity and sense of excitement can be beyond measure.

## Why Non-biblical Biographies?

Why should a pastor, or perhaps a guest preacher, invest an entire sermon in some historical personality, perhaps even a relatively unknown one? Isn't such an effort wasted on a generation said to be disinterested in history and satisfied with everyone getting his or her allotted fifteen minutes of fame?

The answer is quite simple—because nothing is more interesting than people. If you want proof, pause at the checkout counter of your supermarket or chain drug store. Those attention-grabbing periodicals count on *people and personalities* for the vast majority of their headlines. Some of us may smile at the headlines, and many of us may wonder how they stay on the safe side of libel laws. The more honest of us will confess that even when we doubt the substance of the story, we're tempted to pursue it. Our interest is pricked because the articles are about *people*, and people are interesting. Sometimes the headlines grab us even when the particular personality is unknown to us; the potential of the story itself gives excitement to the personality.

Come to think of it; that's the power of gossip. Casual conversation often drags until someone asks, "Have you heard what happened to Bill and Janie?" At that moment the interest quotient rises precipitously. This isn't all bad! Gossip has gotten a worse name than it necessarily deserves. Kathleen Norris reminds us, from her experience after moving back to a small Dakota town, that "gossip done well can be a holy thing. It can strengthen communal bonds."[1] Gossip is sometimes mean, no doubt about it, but gossip exists because people interest us. We care about them. Sometimes we care in unworthy ways, but that doesn't diminish the fact of human interest: it only adds to its mystique.

## A Book about People

Why am I trying to make this point to preachers? The Bible, our basic document, is a book all about *people*. I suspect no book in existence, other than a telephone directory, pays more attention to names than does the Bible. I'm very sure no book portrays human personality more faithfully and more unapologetically. Hermann Gunkel, the great, nineteenth-century scholar, dared to say, the "real greatness of the Hebrew religion" was the Old Testament's "rich and varied gallery of personalities." This distinction is so great, said Gunkel, that "it is an insult to the historical spirit even to name Babylonians and Egyptians in one breath with Israel."[2]

People are not only interesting; they are *instructive*. William McGuffey knew it. More than 120 million copies of his *Eclectic Reader* trained several generations of American children through his clever aphorisms and his stories of great human beings, some famous and some essentially unknown. Henry Wadsworth Longfellow said it best; that's why many of us can still quote him, even if we're troubled by nineteenth-century sexist language:

Lives of great men all remind us
We can make our lives sublime,
And, departing, leave behind us
Footprints on the sands of time.[3]

## Inspiration from Lives of Greatness

"Sublime" was the operative word for Longfellow and probably for McGuffey too. They expected us to find inspiration in the lives of great human beings. I remember such stories from my elementary school days. Nathan Hale regretted that he had but one life to give for his country. Florence Nightingale made nursing a grand profession. Glenn Cunningham had his legs hopelessly burned in a schoolroom fire during his boyhood but went on to become the greatest distance runner of his generation. To mention such persons is to make a particular case for biographical preaching because the list reminds us of the sorry state of the heroic quest in our time. Each year the news media give us some form of a "most admired" list. Each list is an embarrassing declaration of poverty. I won't offer the current list because even if this book is only a year in the publishing, the list will cause you to ask, "Who were they?" That's all the more reason to counter our contemporary poverty with the wealth of the past.

## Dealing with Ambiguity

This is not to suggest that biographical sermons should tell only lovely stories or be starry-eyed in their recitations. To the contrary, part of the value of a good biographical sermon is its willingness to deal with ambiguity. Life is complicated, and we do better in preparing people to live with such ambiguity when we acknowledge that many of our decisions have to be made in gray areas. The Bible never flinches on this issue. The stories of Abraham, Jacob, David, or Simon Peter are uncompromisingly honest—so honest that sometimes we preachers are tempted to skirt around elements of the stories. We should be equally honest when we deal with non-biblical personalities. Eric Liddell's passion was to be a missionary to China, but he also loved to *run.* How could he reconcile what seemed so trivial with what was so grand? Hannah Whitall Smith inspired hundreds of thousands with her book, *The Christian's Secret of a Happy Life,* yet several of her own children notably denied such a life. Faith has to cope with ambiguity, and good biographical preaching gives us an opportunity to work our way through such data. As we do so, we fortify our people with the knowledge that they are not alone in the struggle for fine and consistent living.

Nor must a person have attained fame or true achievement to be a worthy subject of biography. James Boswell's biography of Samuel Johnson is perhaps the most famous biography of all time. Johnson believed that every single life will benefit us if the story is told with complete honesty. We are encouraged in our own living as we see the difficulties people face and how they surmount them.[4] This is true whether the subject is historically famous or the person next door. Sometimes, in fact, the story of the person next door reaches us even more effectively than stories of notables, simply because we find it easier to relate to persons whose life style or level of recognition or achievement seems closer to our own.

## Suggestions for Preaching Biography

It's crucial in this kind of sermon that the story has a point. We expect the subject of the story to be interesting in his or her own right, but if the story deserves a place in the pulpit, it ought also to lead to some internal decision and/or external action by the hearers. They should want to work harder, act more nobly, change their thought patterns, be a better spouse, parent, child, or friend, or take hold of life in some new and responsible way. On the other hand, sometimes it's enough that people walk away feeling they understand life just a little bit better and, as a result, are more ready to cope. In some cases this may mean being able to laugh at themselves a bit on the basis of what they've seen in the life of some other human being. Nevertheless, the story should have a point; it should be more than simply the conveying of information.

The point should be made winsomely. Longfellow's word is significant: these lives should *remind* us. If the sermon becomes too heavy-handed, thoughtful listeners feel insulted that we don't trust their intelligence to reach a conclusion for themselves. The dozens of television commercials we watch every evening have taught us how to connect the dots between the story on the screen and the product decision. Mind you, I'm not suggesting that the biographical sermon should mute the call to decision. I'm only urging that the point should not be in a "now here's the moral of our story" mode.

The story ought also to have some elements of drama. Of course, the drama should be true to the facts and not be overdone. The drama is almost assuredly in every story because one doesn't achieve very much in life without confronting opposition, misunderstanding, and probably some resentment from friends and supporters and the public in general.

## No Synthetic Saints

I want to repeat what I touched upon earlier. Don't make the story an act of hagiography, an idealized biography that turns the human subject into a perfect saint. Biblical writers never did this, so why should we? Our spiritual ancestors in the scriptures have been delivered to us in all their humanness. We know that Abraham lied about Sarah to protect his own life and that Moses lost his virtue of meekness in a moment of irritation. A number of the psalmists despaired of God's faithfulness. The Bible doesn't give us synthetic saints, and we shouldn't do so with personalities from later history.

In choosing subjects for biographical preaching, it's generally better to avoid living persons. I hate to belabor the painfully obvious; but as long as people are living, there's always a chance they will embarrass us. The embarrassment may not come necessarily from a true failing but from the media's vested interest in disaster and in looking for flaws imaginary, perceived, or real. Distance not only lends enchantment, it also gives perspective. When necessary, distance aids the process of understanding and forgiveness.

## Know Your Facts

In your treatment of historical personalities, be as certain as possible of your facts. This means using more than one source. Steve Weinberg, a newspaper reporter who turned to writing biographies, recalls that as a teenager he read autobiographies uncritically. As he began doing research, he discovered that even some of the most notable persons are inclined to omit significant details of their lives. I'm not suggesting that you go muckraking. In some instances the omitted details don't add to our understanding of the person; they only indicate a choice of emphasis. The path you're pursuing in the sermon may lead another way.

In this process of research, you will want especially to get background information on the times. A casual reference to some corollary political, economic, or popular event (sports or entertainment, for instance) adds so much color to the story. To say simply, "This was the year that Babe Ruth set his sixty-home-run record" gives a point of interest to a sports fan. Or, "People were still reveling in stories of the victory at San Juan Hill." Only two or three persons in your audience may identify with such a detail, but it's the kind of detail that colors the material delightfully, just as a touch in a painting or a symphony adds immeasurably for those who know the difference. In our attempt to make our material accessible to everyone, we should never forget the capacities of those who hunger for more. Persons will stop after church to say, "I didn't think anyone else was even interested in that fact."

This means that you must take advantage of standard reference works. Give yourself an hour some afternoon in the reference section of a city library. You will be astonished at the wealth of information waiting to be mined! I won't even attempt to list possible sources because new materials come out every month.

If you know enough about your subject to put together a comprehensible question, you'll find that reference librarians love to help. Not only are they paid to do so, it's in finding answers for your questions that they sense their vocational worth. Give them a chance to think well of themselves—and don't forget to thank them! Now, of course, the Internet offers resources quite literally at our fingertips. You may know more about that than I, however, so I won't attempt to suggest ways and means. In truth, those ways and means expand daily, if not hourly.

## Observe Anniversaries

In choosing to preach biographically, be aware of anniversary dates. Watch especially for centennials and bicentennials. *The Oxford Book of Days* will take you all through the year, giving you more information about each day than you will be able to use. Various writers' almanacs are helpful. The anniversary of some historical event or the centennial of someone's birth, death, or conversion makes the perfect launching point for the sermon. The calendar is always full of dates that can set a preacher's homiletical juices flowing if only the preacher knows about these dates. This is true whether the dates are related to the life of an individual or to the history of a nation, a movement, or a denomination.

I used to feel you should probably avoid preaching biographical sermons around denominational personalities. I've changed my mind. I suspect the times have changed too. I happen to be a United Methodist. It seems to me that in my earlier years in the ministry, a majority of my people knew the names of John and Charles Wesley and a fair number also knew something about Francis Asbury. That's no longer necessarily true. The percentage of those who know is much smaller than it used to be, and the breadth and depth of what they know is much less.

Our people ought to know more about their spiritual ancestors. One might well approach a sermon in just that fashion as many people are into genealogical research these days. For some, it's simply the thing to do. We can cash in on this mood by applying that principle to our spiritual heritage. Occasionally some clergy object to this emphasis on the grounds that we need to pursue ecumenicity, not denominational roots. I reason that any ecumenicity that ignores denominational roots is like a marriage that wants to forget its in-laws. We need to know who we are if we hope to establish true ecumenicity.

A pastor for whom I have particular regard, did a series in 2003 to celebrate the three hundredth anniversary of the birth of John Wesley. He began with several biblical personalities in chronological order demonstrating characteristics of the Christian life as he felt Methodist doctrine defines it. He moved to the stories of John and Charles Wesley, founders of the Methodist movement, and then to the persons who led the German pietistic revival out of which the

Evangelical and United Brethren denominations came. This was particularly important in his setting, because his congregation had been Evangelical United Brethren before the merger with the Methodist Church in 1969.

## An Eye to the Lesser-known

Remember to keep an eye open for some of the lesser-known persons in your faith heritage. Some of the most exciting people (and often, some of the most irregular) are persons who have only a footnote in the standard texts. Trace the footnote, and you may come up with a story that will excite both you and the people to whom you preach. This is particularly true when these persons are not persons of the cloth. People expect us to tell stories about clergy and saints, so they're happily surprised when we choose instead to speak of people who lived out their faith in other walks of life. Indeed, this is one of the key strengths of sermons built around biographies. When I told the story of Johann Sebastian Bach I discovered that I got a unique hearing among a certain segment of my congregation. When they discovered the kind of believer Bach was, they suddenly had a whole new respect for the virtues of the Christian life. Bach made godliness more real to them than John Wesley could, simply because of their predilection toward Bach. As they saw it, John Wesley was a member of the clergy and therefore unlike them. Bach, however, was a composer whose works they had long admired without thinking of him as a fellow believer.

The same kind of case can be made, for instance, for Blaise Pascal. Every congregation has students of science who know Pascal's name, but who know nothing of his transforming religious experience or of the depth of his passion for Christ. Another example is Hildegard of Bingen. Some students of music will know her name, as will people who look for notable feminine personalities. Because of their personal feeling of connection with such persons, listeners may see the Christian faith with different eyes and with greater empathy than they have felt in the past.

## Avoiding the Well-known

In most cases, I would avoid individuals so well known that their appeal may be limited: George Washington or Abraham Lincoln, for instance. Still, if you can bring together enough specifically religious data about such a person—data not easily available to the average person—you will get a very good hearing. Be sure, however, that the material you get is historically sound and has enough real content to carry your point about this person's Christian life or witness.

With only a little effort, you can give additional beauty and meaning to your sermon by music, bulletin inserts, or special displays. For someone such as Bach or Hildegard, some of their music should be part of the service. A line sketch of the person might be included in the order of worship or on the bulletin cover. For authors, prepare a table of their books; for a scientist, set up some display representing his or her work. The possibilities are almost endless if we give ourselves to some creative thinking and planning. Enlist able persons within the congregation to help. They can put their special knowledge or gifts to use, and they will probably be able to bring more specific and exciting materials than you or I might find.

## Using Scripture with Biography

Obviously, these sermons are not basically textual or expository. Still, they should have a basis in scripture that is instructive and has integrity; that is, it ought to be "at one" with the subject matter, making a true integration. Sometimes our chosen person has his or her own cherished passage, in which case the text takes care of itself. More often, it will be a matter of your finding a passage that catches the heart of what you perceive this person's life or message to be. Frank William Boreham preached many biographical sermons. In each case he tried to find the text that had especially influenced that person's life, but this isn't always possible. Don't abuse a passage to make a point. Often you will find instances (as in the Anne Bradstreet sermon, for example) where the person's life is a kind of extended illustration of the scriptural passage. You should not bend the text to fit the life; let the connection be as carefully made as in any sermon. Perhaps even greater care should be used simply because of the danger of misuse.

Always remember you are *preaching a sermon*. You're not simply giving a biography, and no matter how interesting the story of the person's life, you shouldn't be satisfied to do so. You intend to leave a *message*. Don't be heavy-handed about it, but remember your mission all through your preparation. You and I are messengers of good news. This type of sermon simply provides another venue for that message. If done well, this kind of sermon will reach some persons in a manner and in a depth that other sermons may fail to reach.

Many of the sermons in this book have been preached at particular times to particular congregations. In several such instances I have given the specific background information. Some of the sermons are adapted from longer talks that I've given in specialized settings. By the same token, you might want to extend the sermon idea into a forty-five minute lecture for a particular educational or social program. In several cases I have written the sermon for this book, wishing I had had opportunity to preach it.

I offer these sermons in the hope they will stimulate your own sense of homiletical insight. In each case I have included some information that may help you see the potential of the calendar, the specifics of the person's life, or the potential of relationship between text and personality. But whatever I have offered is only a beginning— a stimulus I hope—to your own creative genius.

# CHAPTER 1

# Teresa of Avila

## *A Very Irregular Saint*

### Introducing Teresa

Saints have gotten a bad rap, and it's largely because of their admirers. Over the centuries, the saints have been described in language of such perfection that we ordinary sinners find it hard to relate to them.

In truth, the saints are a hardy lot. One doesn't become a saint without a struggle, in most cases a lifelong struggle. Phyllis McGinley, the Pulitzer Prize winning poet, observed in her book on saints that she had become convinced that "it is easier for a flamboyant sinner to achieve heaven than for an ordinary virtuous, complacent" person.[1] A good many saints have proved this, and few have proved it better than the sixteenth-century Spanish nun, Teresa of Jesus, or as she is now familiarly known, Teresa of Avila. Saints and sinners alike have a right to meet Teresa.

### *Basic Background*

Dona Teresa de Ahumada was born in Avila, Spain, on March 28, 1515, to devout Christian parents. Teresa's mother died when Teresa was thirteen years old, and her father placed her in a school administered by Augustinian nuns. She soon found herself drawn to a religious vocation, with the final impulse coming from her reading of the *Letters of St. Jerome*. The young woman committed herself to a religious life and entered a monastery of Carmelite nuns.

In one sense the years that followed reflect the struggles of the interior life, but those familiar with church politics would say that they reflected equally the story of her struggles with religious hierarchy and civil authorities. Teresa proved to be a fierce advocate, but with a soft touch that would have served her well in twenty-first-century politics anywhere in the world.

Three of Teresa's works—*The Life, The Way of Perfection,* and especially, *The Interior Castle*—are still read today in much of the world by Catholics and Protestants alike, particularly by those who seek a more devoted walk with God. She died in 1582, was beatified in 1614, and canonized in 1622. Pope Paul VI declared her a Doctor of the Church in 1970. She was the first woman to be so named.

### Communities of Interest

At one time only Roman Catholics were interested in saints and their writings. This is no longer the case. Contemporary Protestants may evidence as much interest in the pursuit of "the deeper life" and those who have attained it, as do conventional Catholics. This interest is not limited to a particular segment of the Protestant community. Nevertheless, a sermon on a saint may call for something of a selling job. The likely time for such a sermon, of course, is All Saints Sunday. But since Teresa's birthday comes during a typical Lenten season, one might well include such a sermon as part of the Lenten call to piety and renewed earnestness. I can also imagine a series of perhaps four sermons dealing with a variety of saints from a fairly broad Christian community, including both those who have been canonized and those who have not, Protestants as well as Catholics.

**SERMON** _____

# Teresa of Avila: *A Very Irregular Saint*

## Scripture Lesson: Psalm 5:1–12

Novelists sometimes tell us that it's easy to portray an interesting sinner but that good people tend to be boring. For that reason they prefer to deal with villains. I understand what these writers are saying, but I always have a feeling that they haven't read the Bible very well. This document that we sometimes call "the Good Book" knows more about human frailty and flat-out cussedness than any novelist or playwright can ever hope to duplicate. Goodness isn't easy to come by, and even the best examples of goodness are badly smudged with unpleasant stuff.

## An Irregular Saint

No one demonstrates this fact better than a sixteenth-century nun known today as Teresa of Avila. She is one of the towering figures of Roman Catholic spiritual and institutional history, the first woman ever to be named a Doctor of the Church. But she is a very irregular saint. I add the word "very," because nearly all saints are irregular, but Teresa was especially so.

Because saints tend to be irregular, I had a particular problem in choosing a scripture lesson for the message, the problem of abundance. What scripture fits best? Shall it be something from Paul, who so often revealed his humanness? Or perhaps Peter, who did the same, and usually in fortissimo. Or how about Jeremiah, who wanted to give up preaching. Or Jonah, who ran from God. Or the beloved apostle John, who wanted to call down fire on those who disagreed with him?

Well, I settled on one of the Psalms, one attributed to King David, who was himself quite an irregular person. In this Psalm, David shows his impatience with God but also his trust. He describes his enemies in vehement language and wishes them the worst misfortunes; then he confirms the importance of righteous living and prays God's blessing on those who seek righteousness. Like so many Psalms, this one is a roller coaster of emotions.

The Psalms portray life in all its complexity. Indeed, all the Bible does this because the Bible describes life as it is, not as we might wish it to be. Even that most beloved Psalm, the twenty-third, with its green pastures and still waters, acknowledges that one has to deal with enemies. The Bible is a wonderfully honest book, so it pictures its finest persons in fully candid shots.

## Introducing Teresa

But let me tell you about Teresa of Avila. She was born in 1515, in Avila, Spain, fifth in a family of eleven. When she was thirteen years old her mother died, and soon thereafter her father placed her in a school for girls run by Augustinian nuns. In a period of illness (one of many, all through her life), Teresa recuperated in the country home of her uncle, Don Pedro de Cepeda, a deeply spiritual man. As he read to her regularly from the *Letters of St. Jerome,* Teresa began to feel a call. In spite of her father's opposition, she entered a monastery of Carmelite nuns.

Throughout Teresa's life, beginning even before she entered the Carmelite order, she was passionate in her search for God. As she wrote in a book on her life, "the soul is not satisfied with anything less than God." Her early days as a nun gave no hint of the kind of mystical experiences that would come later. Teresa envied those who wept while they prayed, because she experienced no such easy response. One would never have imagined that Teresa would later be known for her experiences of "locutions" (hearing of words spoken by God) or for instances where, according to legend, her body levitated in the midst of her prayers or in the receiving of Holy Communion.

## Teresa's Suffering

Almost everyone who attains a higher quality of faith suffers some measurable adversity. It may be defeat or failure, betrayal by friend or family, profound psychological trauma, or great physical distress. For Teresa, it was the latter. Fairly early in her training as a nun, she became seriously ill. At the time the popular form of alternative medicine was the *curandera,* a woman who worked with herbal remedies often involving a regimen of purges. The one who treated Teresa had her vomiting uncontrollably, with daily purging. When she went into a cataleptic state, the nuns thought she was dying. They prepared her for burial, wrapping her in a shroud and sealing her eyelids with wax. After four days she suddenly awoke and asked for the opportunity to confess.

Biographers have speculated the nature of Teresa's illness, giving virtually every imaginable diagnosis. Some speak of the severe dehydration she suffered, some of a possible thyroid problem, others of malaria, heart disease, cerebral meningitis, and of course, severe neurosis. A recent biographer, Cathleen Medwick, observes that "spirituality can coexist with neurosis, as can intellectual clarity, business acumen, and common sense."[2] Whatever the illness, it was severe enough that Teresa could not move for eight months, and it was three years before she could crawl.

One thing is sure, the illness must have added to the toughness of Teresa's soul and body. In the years that followed, she rose indomitably over every kind of stress and struggle. One thinks immediately of her frequent, almost continuous physical pain. One time when her face ached, her throat hurt, and she suffered a severe pain in her side, she wrote a trusted friend, "Any one of these ailments would have been enough to kill me if God had been pleased to desire it, but apparently He is not about to do me that favor."[3]

Late in her life, she fell down a flight of stairs on a Christmas Eve when she misjudged a step. Doctors set the broken left arm, but it healed badly, so a *curandera* was brought in to re-break it for resetting. As a result, Teresa was never able to use the arm again. A dedicated lay sister attended her for the rest of her life, dressing her and assisting in even the simplest tasks. As if the illnesses themselves were not enough, she traveled almost constantly under conditions that would break a strong body.

## Teresa's Accomplishments

I suspect that for Teresa, intense as she was, one of life's greatest trials was to maintain patience with those of lesser commitment. Over the years she established seventeen houses. Most of the nunneries at the time were reasonably comfortable, some very much so. She ran a tighter regimen and instituted reforms with a vigor that brought frequent resentment. Absolute silence was not required, but she forbid gossiping and babbling. Food was simple: poultry once a week and ordinarily a little bread, cheese, and fruit, with occasional fish or an egg. If no food was available, the sisters nevertheless assembled at the table to find their nourishment in fellowship and in the love of God. Time was never wasted.

## Teresa's Faith

Through all her life, Teresa sought for confessors who could lead her into a closer walk with God. Unfortunately, few priests had a faith advanced enough to give Teresa the challenge she sought. The larger leadership of the Catholic Church in Spain was marked more often by the search for position and preferment than by the search for God. They often saw Teresa as a threat. Her mystical experiences were easily misunderstood, especially because she was a woman in a time and culture where men were considered innately superior. Felipe Sega, the papal nuncio, described her as "an unstable, restless, disobedient, and contumacious female."[4]

I'm sure that to a conservative administrator, Teresa did seem unstable and without a doubt, she was restless. As for disobedience, one could hardly be as visionary as Teresa without appearing disobedient to those who wanted things to remain essentially as they were. As for being contumacious, I suspect this judgment is in the eye of the beholder. In truth, it appears that Teresa often conducted herself in such a way as to make men feel that they were her superiors. It's not too difficult to make people think they're superior when they are already predisposed to that position.

## Teresa's World of Action

From all evidence, Teresa did not want to be an administrator. She preferred to dedicate herself to prayer and the pursuit of sanctity. Dag Hammarskjold, Secretary-General of the United Nations from 1953 until his death in 1961 and perhaps the greatest person to serve in that role, wrote, "In our era, the road to holiness necessarily passes through the world of action."[5]

Like it or not, Teresa may have demonstrated Hammarskjold's conviction for her own day, and apparently she didn't like it. She confesses that she was "on the verge of complaining" when she advised God to either stop ordering her to take on so many projects or help her to get them done. In truth, she *did* get them done, but I suspect that, restless and energetic as she was, she constantly saw new things that needed to be done. If God laid constant tasks upon Teresa it is because she so constantly stationed herself where the task was waiting.

## Teresa's Candor

I don't know what it would have been like to have worked with, for, or in supervision of Teresa of Avila, but I'm sure I would have enjoyed her sense of humor. She was as candid with God as the writers of the Book of Psalms but with more of a twinkle in her eye. As strict and spare as life was in her nunneries, she insisted on recreation, because she believed it renewed the spirit for prayer. Recreation included singing religious tunes, reading incidental poetry, and dancing. Speaking of dancing, a few days before she entered the Carmelite Convent, a young man admired her feet in their dancing slippers. Teresa answered, "Take a good look, sir. You won't be getting another chance."[6]

As I indicated, Teresa was equally direct with God. Almost everyone has heard of a time when the burdens of her work were more than she could handle. When she complained, God answered that this was the way he treated his friends. Teresa replied, "No wonder You have so few friends when You treat the ones You have so badly."[7] She recorded another instance when she prayed, "Lord, if I had my way that woman wouldn't be Superior here," to which God replied, "Teresa, if I had My way, she wouldn't be, either."[8]

A great part of Teresa's secret, of course, is that she didn't take herself too seriously. She would confess repeatedly that she was a wretched soul whose only claim to virtue was her insistence on reaching God. She loved good food, of which at times she got little. On one occasion while she was enjoying a partridge, someone reprimanded her, and she replied, "There is a time for partridge and a time for penance."[9]

She confessed readily that she was susceptible to praise. "I have no defense against affection. I could be bribed with a sardine." She didn't forget that she was once strikingly attractive–and still compelling in her appearance long after some of her natural beauty was diminished. When she sat for her portrait in 1576, at age 61, she reportedly said to the artist, "God forgive you, Fray Juan, you've made me a bleary-eyed, old hag."

## Teresa's Legacy

I wonder how she would handle what has happened to her reputation and, indeed, her body in the centuries following her death. Biographers report that her right foot and upper jaw are in Rome, and a bit of her cheek in Madrid. Other parts of her body are in Brussels, Paris, and Mexico, and of course, at San Jose de Avila, the first convent she founded. Her left hand has traveled far. General Francisco Franco, Spain's redoubtable dictator from 1936 until shortly before his death in 1975, kept the hand beside him until his death. I think Teresa would have found all this amusing

Six years after Teresa's death, the first edition of her writings was published. They are still widely read today. She was beatified in 1614 and canonized in 1622. The papal bull praised her for "overcoming... her female nature." As a man, I'm not able to judge what this means, though I'm suspicious that as presented in the bull, it was probably a backhanded compliment. I only know that if this overcoming is anything like overcoming one's male nature, it is a huge victory and is full evidence that one is, for sure, a bona fide saint.

CHAPTER 2

# John Robinson

*The Preacher Who Missed
the Boat*

## Introducing John Robinson

John Robinson intrigues me. Perhaps it's because I believe so much in the power of the pulpit. It's possible that I put so much stock in this belief that I give Robinson a larger place than he deserves. Nevertheless, I can't help feeling that more attention should be paid to this ancestor of America who never got to our shores.

Robinson was pastor to the people who landed on Plymouth Rock in 1620. As such, he enjoys a particular tie to all those persons who claim to have had ancestors on the Mayflower. He sent off a large share of his congregation with the expectation he would eventually join them, but he died before that opportunity came. Nevertheless, he made his imprint on this country. He did so not only in the broad ways that we preachers always hope we're influencing people, but also in the specifics of the sermon he preached to his people before their departure. In fact, he made his imprint through all the sermons prior to that sailing and in his correspondence during the four or five years following.

### Basic Background

John Robinson was born at Sturton-le-Steeple in 1575. He received bachelor's (1596) and master's degrees (1599) at Corpus Christi College, Cambridge. An active leader in the Puritan branch of the

19

Church of England, he gradually joined the more extreme Puritans who chose to separate from the church, feeling that the Church of England was fatally corrupt. He joined the separatist congregation at Scrooby and in time became their minister. In their search for freedom, the group immigrated to the Netherlands, first to Amsterdam, then to Leiden. He died in 1625, some five years after seeing a portion of his congregation head to the new world.

### Communities of Interest

John Robinson's story is, of course, of interest to anyone who loves American history, even in a superficial way. He appeals especially to those with ties to New England and to those with Congregational roots. His story can be especially appealing on the Sunday before Thanksgiving, the Sunday near Independence Day, or perhaps the Sunday before a national election. There are also reasons to think of him on the Sunday in November that is celebrated as Bible Sunday.

## SERMON

# John Robinson: *The Preacher Who Missed the Boat*

## Scripture Lesson: Psalm 119:9–16

If you're part of any Christian body in America, Protestant or Catholic or Orthodox, I want to identify an ancestor for you. The line of descent is closer if you're a Protestant, and the line is direct if you're in the Congregational tradition; but everyone in the American Christian family has something of a tie to a seventeenth-century minister named John Robinson, even though, he never made it to our shores.

### Robinson's Background

John Robinson was born well over four hundred years ago, in 1575, in England. He was a lover of learning and set himself to getting a fine education, earning a bachelor's and a master's degree from Corpus Christi College of England's great Cambridge University. Above all he was a person of deep religious conviction, a devout and active Puritan.

At that time, most Puritans were part of the Church of England, working for reform within the church. But there were some in the

Puritan movement who felt the Church of England was "fatally corrupt," so they chose to separate themselves from it entirely. Rather than working for reform from within, they chose to remove their witness and work from without. They were known, not surprisingly, as "Separatists."

John Robinson's religious convictions led him, around 1605, to leave the established church and become part of this movement. In truth, such a decision was pretty well forced on him. He was one of the three hundred clergy that came under a decree of the Hampton Court Conference depriving them of office for their disagreements with the Church of England.

He joined the Separatist congregation at Scrooby, and after a time became their minister. He was referred to in his own time as "that famous and worthy man." George Willison says that he was "the most beloved and respected" of the early Puritans, "a man of genuine distinction in an age of great men."[1]

## Robinson on the Move

The people with whom Robinson associated himself valued their faith above everything else in their lives. Nurturing that faith was their primary concern. With this in mind, they left England in 1608 for the Netherlands, settling briefly in Amsterdam, then moving on to the city of Leiden. As time passed, however, they encountered a series of concerns with life in the Netherlands and decided their best course was to immigrate to the new, unknown land of America. In September, 1620, forty-one people from the congregation set sail for America, being joined in England with a somewhat motley group of sixty-one other people from in and around London.

But John Robinson, their pastor, couldn't make the trip with them. He felt he should remain with the larger group from their body who were remaining in the Netherlands. He hoped to join his congregation in America as soon as possible. As it turned out, he died five years later, before he could fulfill his dream. So he never became part, directly, of our American story.

## Preparing for America

As the group prepared to leave Leiden and their pastor, they met for a "day of solemn humiliation." After a time of earnest prayer, Robinson spoke. He took his text, from a similar occasion, the time when the people of Israel were preparing for their journey from captivity back to Jerusalem. The text, Ezra 8:21, reads: "Then I proclaimed a fast there, at the river Ahava, that we might deny ourselves before our God, to seek from him a safe journey for ourselves, our children, and all our possessions."

The people remembered especially their pastor's closing words. He acknowledged that they could not say whether they would live to see one another again. Of course, as it happened, this was their last meeting with Robinson. Then, with the humility that apparently was characteristic of John Robinson, he charged the people "to follow him no further than he followed Christ. And if God should reveal any thing to us by any other instrument of his, to be as ready to receive it, as ever we were to receive any truth from his ministry: For he was very confident the Lord had more truth and light yet to break forth out of his Holy Word."[2]

No one can estimate the impact of Robinson's message on his little band of Pilgrims. I'm sure they heard him with particular intensity–inevitably the case with farewell words. A sermon or a conversation that might be taken somewhat casually at a routine time will carry much greater impact in the context of a parting scene.

But more than that, the Puritans who were to set out for the new world the next day were a people with a sense of destiny. They weren't coming to America for a new economic opportunity, or even for the establishing of a political entity. For them, America represented a chance to begin something new and great for God. They expected to build a community that could be an example to the whole world. They saw themselves as a new Israel, God's people for a new day. It isn't by chance that Robinson chose the text from Ezra 8. For the Pilgrims, their journey was also a release from a land of captivity. While going to America was not a return to their homeland, in a spiritual sense they must have seen it as such. If America gave them the opportunity to worship without government interference and if they could fulfill their sense of mission in establishing a household of God, then their new home would, indeed, be a new Jerusalem.

## The Pilgrim Story

As it turned out, the Pilgrim band needed all the help they could get. You know the story, in some version or other, from your grade school days. Some of the group died during the Atlantic crossing, and even more died during the hard first winter. At times the sick outnumbered the able-bodied. They were without a pastor, so their spiritual sustenance had to come from one another.

One wonders especially what the people thought of Robinson's parting words. What of this "more truth and light yet to break forth" from God's Word? After all, this was a conservative body of people, perhaps the most conservative in their day. They were a people who found their roots and their boundaries in the scriptures. They weren't inclined to treat scripture casually, and I'm sure they didn't think their pastor was recommending such treatment. Their attitude toward the Bible was a seventeenth-century reflection of Psalm 119. That Psalm—the longest chapter in our Bible—dedicates its 176 verses to the praise of God's Word: that portion that we now refer to as the Pentateuch, which Judaism calls the Torah, the Law of God.

## Robinson and the Word of God

John Robinson believed the Word of God was perfect, but he knew that he was not, and neither were his people. God's Word contained more than he had yet been able to teach them, more than they had been able to absorb. Beyond that, it is clear that Robinson was confessing his own limits of knowledge. He was a truly humble man. Humility is no small achievement for any of us, but it is a particularly impressive virtue when it is combined with deep, religious convictions. A person with convictions he or she is willing to die for, holds those convictions with intensity, but that intensity can easily slip over into pride. I am impressed that John Robinson believed so deeply yet had such breadth of spirit.

## Robinson on Church History

Part of Robinson's secret is that he knew a little history and was willing to learn from it. As he told his congregation that yet more light would break forth from the scriptures, he reminded them of what had happened to other Reformed bodies. The Lutherans, he said, "could not be drawn to go beyond what Luther saw, for whatever part of God's will he had further imparted and revealed to Calvin, they [the Lutherans] will rather die than embrace it." So too, Robinson said, with the followers of Calvin; "They stick fast where he left them." This was a "misery," he said, "for though they were precious shining lights in their times, yet God had not revealed his whole will to them."[3]

Robinson's words provide magnificent counsel, not only for religious bodies, but equally for political bodies and for every reform movement. It is often noted that the reformers of one generation are the standpatters of the next and the reactionaries of the third. It's difficult for the children of immigrants to feel compassion for the new generation of immigrants. It's hard for a respected denomination to remember that it was once a despised sect and to look thoughtfully on the new sect that may be rising to assume its own place in the company of denominations. So I marvel at John Robinson, a man whose convictions ran deep and who was willing to pay the price of his convictions, but who nevertheless maintained a heart for those who differed with him.

## Robinson and Tolerance

I'm especially impressed with this little bit of common sense. Robinson explains that for the most part we're inclined to be for or against tolerance and diversity in religion, depending on the situation. "Protestants living in the country of Papists [that is, Catholics] commonly plead for toleration of religion; so do Papists that live where Protestants bear sway, though few of either, especially of the clergy as they are called, would have the other tolerated where the world goes on their side."[4] I described that as "common sense," but of course it is quite uncommon. That's why on college campuses students and sometimes faculty plead for freedom of speech until the speech violates their own pet prejudice; then they think it should be shut down.

It is very difficult to have deep convictions, yet maintain an empathetic spirit. Mind you, I'm not impressed by people who claim to have an open mind but who have no convictions upon which to close their mind. Openness itself accomplishes very little in our world. People who achieve, whether in religion, politics, philosophy, or business, achieve on the strength of their convictions. Those who achieve best learn also to listen to the mind of others and to respect the opinions of others, even when they disagree with those opinions. John Robinson apparently succeeded in maintaining such a spirit. In his later years he was often grieved by the harsh judgments of some of his Pilgrim colleagues.

## Robinson's Congregation in America

His little American congregation survived their first winter, though it must have seemed they would never make it. I don't think I'm being naïve or sentimental when I suggest that one of the reasons they survived was because Robinson had taught them to feed faithfully on the scriptures. Like the poet who wrote Psalm 119, they could say, "I will meditate on your precepts, / and fix my eyes on your ways" (Ps. 119:15). Faced daily by death and starvation, they needed to fix their eyes on the ultimate. They found that ultimate in the scriptures.

In all I have said thus far, I have emphasized John Robinson's role as a leader who may have influenced the new nation that was about to be born at Plymouth Rock. It's easy to give such an emphasis because I picture the Mayflower group drawing up the Mayflower

Compact, which began, "In the name of God, Amen," and which declared that they would covenant together "into a civill body politick." In a very real sense that document can be called a crucial ancestor of our Declaration of Independence and our Constitution.

The Mayflower Compact was a start toward sound and structured government for free women and men. It wasn't the end of the story, but it was a substantial beginning. It came from people who had gotten their theological foundation from that good and able man, John Robinson. It's not surprising they said they would "covenant" together. This was the language of a biblical people. What they were doing they saw themselves as doing under the hand of God and with the hope that it would glorify God.

## Robinson and the People's Needs

But when I think of Robinson encouraging his people to expect yet "more truth and light" to break forth from God's Word, I remind myself that Robinson wasn't thinking primarily of governments and institutions. As a pastor, he was thinking more particularly of the daily needs of his people. I would be presumptuous to venture far into Robinson's thoughts, so what I am about to say may never have occurred to him. I want only to submit that the Pilgrims needed "more truth and light" as they came to their new life in New England.

Our knowledge of the Bible and its effectiveness in our lives is always set within the context of our need and our perceptiveness at the time of our reading. That is, in old England and in the Netherlands, the Pilgrims read the scriptures within the context of life as they knew it there. This perception was wonderfully fulfilling for that setting; but in the new world of America, set amidst new perils and new possibilities, a new understanding was needed. They would need for new light to break forth from God's Word.

Let me put it in a personal way. As an eleven-year-old, I was blessed by encouragement from a Presbyterian evangelist who came to our little Methodist Church. He gave me a method for reading through the entire Bible in a year. I promptly set myself to do so and read through the Bible as an eleven-year-old. It was a remarkable, transforming year. I'm no longer a sixth- and seventh-grader, in the world of the 1930s. What the Bible did for me then is not sufficient for me now. I am a different person, because of the passage of many years and the accumulating of many experiences, so I need "new light" to break forth from God's Word.

It is always so with all of us. Each year, each week, each day is a new challenge. Yesterday's faith is not enough. We need a new encounter with God for *this* day and for all that it holds. We need new light and truth from God's Word, not new in the sense of novelty, but new in the sense of this-day reality. You and I need to live for God today! If we are to do so effectively and winsomely, we will need reality from God this day, the kind of reality to be found in communion with God and through the scriptures.

I'd like to have known John Robinson. I would like to have his depth of conviction blended with his breadth of understanding. I would like for him to lead me, as a believer and as a citizen, as I seek for yet "more truth and light" from God's Word.

# CHAPTER 3

# The King James Bible
## A Committee That Succeeded

### Introducing the King James Bible

Does the King James Bible deserve a place in a collection of biographical sermons? Without a doubt! Like the Magna Charta, the Declaration of Independence, or the Constitution of the United States, the King James Bible has a life of its own and deserves that its story should be told. When it comes to the extent and pervasiveness of a document's reach, it can easily be argued that the King James Bible has had a life of its own, beyond that of the political documents I have mentioned.

The story of the King James Bible is compelling. It contains an amount of intrigue, of political shenanigans, of grand scholarship, and of influence that will exist as long as our planet is inhabited. It stands as an element of devotion and piety and with occasional miracles that will inspire all but the most jaded.

*Basic Background*

As with any other biography, the King James Bible has its ancestry, not only in the Hebrew and Greek Scriptures, but also in translations that preceded it. The King James Version relied heavily on Tyndale's earlier work and on the Geneva Bible. Some scholars also see points at which the King James translation followed patterns established by Martin Luther in his translation into vernacular German.

The work on the King James translation began in 1604 after a call from King James I and was completed in 1611. It has served for generations as the Authorized Version, a title it retains in England even today. The marketplace in English Bibles has seen a wide variety of new translations in the past fifty years. Still the KJV retains a dedicated following–partly of those who feel it is still the only "authorized" version and partly of those who love the beauty of its cadences.

### Communities of Interest

Almost everyone who knows anything about the Bible in English translations–even the many who know very little–has some familiarity with the King James Version. For some the mystique makes the story interesting. Others are simply curious about a book that is so familiar and so beloved, yet about which they know very little except that it is "the Holy Bible." I have told this story in various forms in a rather wide variety of places and have always found the audience more interested than my talents deserve.

The story provides a good theme for what is known in many congregations as "Bible Sunday" at the beginning of National Bible Week in mid-November. A pastor might also tell this story on the Sunday when Bibles are presented to the members of the Sunday school or youth group. The theme is appropriate even if another translation is presented, since the King James Bible is still the most familiar version for a substantial part of our population. If another version is being presented, the King James story may lead into a summary regarding more recent translations.

**SERMON** _____

# The King James Bible: *A Committee That Succeeded*

## Scripture Lesson: Jeremiah 37:11–17

Almost everyone seems to agree that the present generation is biblically illiterate. Surveys by responsible polling organizations indicate that even people who are faithful church members–and many who testify that they have been "born again"–fall short in elementary biblical knowledge.

## Speaking King James

I'm afraid I'm compelled to agree with this evaluation. Nevertheless, I contend that most persons in America, as well as persons in other parts of the English-speaking world, reflect more knowledge of the Bible than they imagine. I submit that most of us "speak" the Bible—specifically, the King James Version of the Bible—without knowing how often we do so.

Let me make my point by putting together a portion of an imaginary conversation. Imagine your friend saying, "This afternoon I was in a meeting of *the powers that be* in our organization—*salt of the earth* people, even though most of them are too busy seeking *filthy lucre* so they can live off the *fat of the land*. Well, as I was driving home from this meeting, suddenly, *in the twinkling of an eye,* I could see the *handwriting on the wall*. It was as *clear as crystal;* I was headed for an accident that might be the end. But just then, I escaped, by *the skin of my teeth!* Thank God! I can't help feeling I must be *the apple of his eye.*"

You get my point. Many of the figures of speech that flavor our day-to-day conversation either originated in the King James Version of the Bible or in the Tyndale translation that preceded it, or were made part of our common speech by their inclusion in the King James Bible. This Bible is in many ways our mother tongue, even today. A generation that is biblically illiterate still "talks Bible," the King James Bible.

## King James Establishing Our Language

Language is an elusive, ephemeral thing until it is put into writing. Even then it continues to be elusive—and also exclusive—until it is available to the masses of people in some relatively established, permanent form. Until that happens, a language remains very regional, so that people in one area may speak very differently from those a relatively short distance away, especially if there is some kind of natural, geographical or political barrier. Furthermore, a nation or a region can be sharply divided between those who read and those who do not, with dramatic differences in language.

It may be hard for you and me to imagine an English-speaking world where the vast majority could not read. But that's the way it was in the fourteenth, fifteenth, and sixteenth centuries. In truth, some people liked it that way. They enjoyed both the superiority and the power they had over those persons who were illiterate. After all, it's what you know that gives you economic and political mobility. That's why tyrants of any generation want to keep their people in ignorance. In some instances they do so by not allowing people to read, and in other instances by legislating what is available to be read.

## John Wycliffe

On the other hand, throughout history we've had persons who wanted the whole world to read. John Wycliffe (1320?–1384) is one of the grandest examples. He may well have been the most learned man of his generation in England. At age 48, he came to a conclusion that was revolutionary for his time that the Bible must be the sole law of the Church. From the base of that conviction, he argued that there must be a translation that would be accessible to the humblest person for reading and learning. So he and his followers began such a translation.

His teachings were heretical to the Catholic Church of that time, but he was allowed to die in peace. Forty-four years later, however, Bishop Richard Fleming exhumed Wycliffe's remains, burned them, and threw the ashes into the Swift River.

## William Tyndale

Then there was William Tyndale. David Daniell, for many years a professor of English in the University of London, says no other Englishman, including Shakespeare, has reached so many people. Born around 1494, Tyndale earned bachelor's and master's degrees at Oxford. He developed a passionate conviction that the common people should have the Bible. He declared his position memorably in "the company of a learned man." "If God spare my life," Tyndale said, "ere many years I will cause a boy that driveth the plough shall know more of the Scripture than thou dost."[1]

It was a magnificent statement, not only for those of us who love the Bible but for anyone who believes in universal education. The statement threw down the gauntlet, because in time, Tyndale paid for it with his life.

### Tyndale's New Testament

Other scholars, unfortunately, weren't sympathetic with Tyndale's vision, but a wealthy merchant, Humphrey Monmouth, was. He had heard Tyndale preach. He tried at first to help him with his project in England. It soon became clear that they faced too much opposition there, so Tyndale continued his translation of the New Testament into English in Germany, and the first English New Testament was printed there. A little later, Tyndale made Antwerp his headquarters. Monmouth—God bless him—did the financing.

Let me mention that some others had translated the Bible into English before Tyndale, but he was the first to produce a printed version, thus making the Bible widely available. That was, of course, his mission. Also, the other translations had been from the Latin, while Tyndale went back to the original languages, Hebrew and Greek, for his translations.

## Tyndale's Mission

But above all, Tyndale's genius was for the ploughboy. Tyndale himself was so skilled in seven languages (Hebrew, Greek, Latin, Italian, Spanish, English, and French) that one of his contemporaries said that whichever he spoke, you might think it his native tongue. Still Tyndale was aiming not for scholars but for what we today might call the person on the street. He worked from the realization that the apostles, in their day, had delivered the message in the language of the people (what we now call *koine* Greek, the common language of home and marketplace). Tyndale wanted the people of England to have the message in their mother tongue. He aimed for simple, direct sentences and idiomatic use of words. Yet with it all, he didn't allow his translation to be crude or cheap. As Professor Daniell said, "Tyndale was writing for ordinary men and women reading the Greek New Testament in English to themselves, to each other, round the table, in the parlor, under the hedges, and in the fields."[2]

## Tyndale's Opposition

The Bishop of London was so afraid of Tyndale's translation that he commissioned a man named Packington to scour the continent for copies. Packington went directly to Tyndale to buy his inventory. When Tyndale learned that the purchaser was the Bishop of London and that the Bishop would, of course, burn the Bibles, he answered, "I am the gladder, for these two benefits shall come thereof: I shall get money from him for these books and bring myself out of debt, and the whole world shall cry out on the burning of God's Word, and the overplus of the money that shall remain to me shall make me more studious to correct the said New Testament, and so newly to imprint the same once again; and I trust the second will much better like you than ever did the first."[3]

## Tyndale's Last Days

Eventually, of course, Tyndale was captured. A fellow Englishman, Henry Phillips, betrayed him, leading him to the place where he could be arrested. Tyndale spent the next eighteen months near Brussels in the dark cell of a castle prison. In October, 1536, still in his early forties, he was publicly strangled and his body burned.

He had known, perhaps from the outset of his project, that this would likely be his end. No matter! He was accomplishing the work to which he had dedicated himself. In truth, he accomplished more than he could ever have dreamed in his wildest imagination.

## Authorizing the King James Version

But why am I telling you so much about William Tyndale, when my subject is the King James Bible? Well, stay with me, and I'll tell you.

On Monday, January 16, 1604, King James I brought to the palace at Hampton Court a small group of clergy. By this time the church in England—what we now call the Anglican Church—had separated from the Catholic Church and was dealing with problems of its own. They opposed the Puritans, a group within the Anglican Church who were seeking to "purify" the church and to invigorate its spirituality. King James hoped to establish some common ground between the two parties.

It proved to be an interesting day and an eternally surprising one in its outcome. At one point, James said he would "harry" the Puritans out of the land. Nevertheless, he chose to lean their direction again and again in the course of the discussions. This may reflect his years of dealing with them while he was still James VI of Scotland. Some historians have described this son of Mary, Queen of Scots, as having only one devout belief: kingcraft. Thirty-seven at the time of this meeting and spluttering when he spoke because his tongue was large for his mouth, he was in truth something of a biblical scholar. Like Queen Elizabeth before him, he wrote poetry from the Psalms and, in a surprising turn, wrote a commentary on the Book of Revelation.

His aim at this point was to keep a united nation, and the clergy were essential to any such hope. Somewhere in the proceedings, John Rainolds—a Puritan, and in the judgment of some, the finest scholar in England at the time—suggested a new translation of the Bible. James agreed. The Bible then in common use in England was the Geneva Bible, and James was uneasy with many of the explanatory notes in this version. As it turned out, the decision to develop a new translation was the only real result of the meeting. It was a side issue, almost an incidental one. But what a side issue!

The product of that side issue is still with us today, in more ways by far than simply the translation itself. As for King James, it is the only thing for which he is remembered. Because of this translation, literally millions of people who know nothing of any other English ruler know the name of King James I.

## The Making of the King James Version

Fifty-four persons—all men—were chosen to make the translation. Although the King authorized the work, he didn't pay for it. The royal budget was in too much trouble at the time. It was therefore necessary to find "livings" for the chosen scholars, that is, clerical appointments of one kind or another that would provide income for them while they were occupied much of the time in their work of scholarship. As far as we can tell, the three institutions where they did their work—Oxford, Cambridge, and Westminster—provided them free board and room while they worked, as well as meeting space.

## The King James Translators

### Dr. Lancelot Andrewes

As far as history is concerned, very few of these fifty-four men have reason to be remembered. Even the number, fifty-four, is uncertain. The best known of the group was Dr. Lancelot Andrewes. Many of his writings are still available today, especially his devotional works. You can estimate his literary ability by the company he kept. He was a close friend in his college years of Edmund Spenser, remembered for *The Fairy Queen.* Francis Bacon, the master essayist, was his friend for twenty years and often sought his advice on writing.

### Laurence Chaderton

John Rainolds, to whom I referred earlier, was the most outstanding Puritan in the group, but his fellow Puritan, Laurence Chaderton, was also outstanding. He converted to Puritanism as a college student, much to his father's distress. His father offered him thirty pounds a year, a very adequate living at the time, to leave Cambridge. "Son Laurence, if you will renounce the new sect which you have joined, you may expect all the happiness which the care of an indulgent father can assure you; otherwise, I enclose a shilling to buy a wallet. Go and beg."[4] Chaderton stayed by his convictions. Here's an interesting sequel: he lived to be 103 and could still read without glasses at age 100.

### Richard Thomson

The fifty-four men proved to be a remarkable committee. No committee ever succeeded more admirably and with more blessed results. But the committee members themselves were an uneven lot. Richard Thomson, born in Holland of English parents and known as "Dutch" Thomson, was said to have seldom gone to bed sober.

## Samuel Ward

Samuel Ward, on the other hand, left behind a diary filled with earnest self-examination. He condemned himself for wandering thoughts in the chapel at prayer time. He repented that some nights he fell asleep without his last thoughts being on God. An earnest, sensitive soul, indeed!

## John Bois

John Bois was raised by a scholarly father who taught him Hebrew when he was only five. The father's passion for learning took full flower in the boy. Bois would go to the university library at four o'clock in the morning and without food break stay until eight o'clock in the evening studying books of medicine. When the rector of Boxworth was about to die, he appealed to Bois to become his successor by marriage to his daughter. Bois was 36 at the time. He evaluated the Boxworth girl and accepted the offer. From their union came four sons and two daughters.

## John Overall

Then there's John Overall, the Dean of St. Paul's. He married a woman of great beauty, Anne Orwell. But Sir John Selby found her beautiful as well and persuaded her to run away with him. A group of men chased them down and brought Anne back to her husband. It was commonly said that they lived thereafter in "holy deadlock."

## George Abbot

While speaking of the remarkable group that made up the translators, the story of George Abbot should be told. When George's mother was pregnant with him, she dreamed that if she could catch and eat a jack or a pike, her child would be a son and would rise to heights of success. One day while she drew water from a nearby river, she trapped a young pike in her pitcher. So she took it home, cooked it, and ate it. Some who heard her story offered to sponsor the boy in his schooling. At sixteen, he entered Balliol College, Oxford. In time he became Bishop of London, and then in 1611 (the year of the King James Version) he was made Archbishop of Canterbury.

Whatever one thinks of his mother's dream, Abbot rose to remarkable heights. A cynic might observe that Abbot did so partly through his readiness to offer inordinate praise to James I. Abbot had also to deal with a very real tragedy: when hunting a decade later, he accidentally shot Peter Harkins, a keeper, in the arm. Harkins bled to death. Thus Abbot has the dubious distinction of being the only translator of the King James Bible to have killed someone.

## Translating the King James Version

How did these fifty-some men go about producing what is commonly called a masterpiece? Mind you, they didn't write the Bible, but they cast it in memorable English, leaving us with phrases that have shaped the English language ever since. The Bible was divided into study portions. Each study portion was assigned to those committee members who were considered strongest in the language in which the portion was written. At their meetings, one scholar would read his translation while others held either a Greek or Hebrew document, or something in French, Italian, Spanish, and so on. Tyndale's or Coverdale's translation was close at hand. As they compared the new rendition with the others, they spoke up if they found fault with their colleague's rendering. If not, he read on.

Their meeting rooms were often bitterly cold, so much so that a person could hardly hold a book or a pen except by staying near the fireplace. They were not paid for their work. They were compelled to work at odd hours, around their other responsibilities. Although they were all able scholars, only Lancelot Andrewes was a master of the English language. They had no Ben Jonson, no Christopher Marlowe, and certainly no William Shakespeare. They did, however, inherit the work of William Tyndale, and it seems fair enough to call him a genius. They had also the work of Miles Coverdale, who deserves honor.

They had something else going for them. As Gustavus Paine has said, "their writing flows with a sense of *must.*" Paine continues, "If the marvel of what they did exceeds even the marvel of Shakespeare, it is because their aim was greater, no less indeed than the salvation of their world."[5]

And they did it in a committee. That seems like a miracle all by itself.

# CHAPTER 4

# Anne Bradstreet

## *A Forgotten Ancestor*

### Introducing Anne Bradstreet

I first met Anne Bradstreet through a college survey course in American literature. Her poetry pleased me. I was impressed by the transparent quality of her faith as well as by the way she used simple words to communicate very real beauty. So when I served as a guest preacher for several summer Sundays in a church in the Congregational tradition, I decided I should introduce the congregation to one of their worthiest ancestors.

### *Basic Background*

Anne (Dudley) Bradstreet was born c. 1612, probably in Northampton, England. At 16 she married Simon Bradstreet and two years later, in 1630, came to America as one of the first settlers on Massachusetts Bay. Her father and her husband would both eventually serve as governors of the colony. A mother of eight children, she wrote her poetry in the midst of the rigors of pioneer life.

Without her knowing it, her brother-in-law took some of her poems to England where they were published in 1650 under the title, *The Tenth Muse Lately Sprung Up in America.* She was one of the first persons to write English verse in America. In 1678, six years after her death, her poems were first published in America as an expanded and enlarged form of the British work, *Several Poems Compiled with Great Variety of Wit and Learning.*

*Communities of Interest*

Anne Bradstreet holds special appeal for persons who love American history, particularly New England history, for lovers of literature, and for persons who enjoy seeing faith communicated in fine, unpretentious poetry. She also offers tacit encouragement to those persons who hope to do creative things but who see themselves as having little opportunity to do so.

## SERMON

# Anne Bradstreet: *A Forgotten Ancestor*

## Scripture Lesson: 2 Corinthians 4:16–18

When we join a church, we inherit a family. This includes more than the local congregation of which we become a part. At its best, such a congregation becomes family, though unfortunately, not always. Along with this new family, we also get a large, extended family through a whole line of spiritual ancestors. We get these ancestors whether we want them or not. The apostle Paul told the people at Corinth that they could lay claim to himself, Apollos, or Cephas (1 Cor. 3:21–22). If he were speaking to us today, he might add Francis of Assisi, Martin Luther, John Wesley, Teresa of Avila, and Billy Sunday. They're all part of the larger community to which we belong through Jesus Christ.

Each one has something special to contribute. I want to tell you about someone whose contribution is unique and far-reaching, yet it's likely you've never realized that she is part of your faith-family. In fact, you may never have heard of her. On the other hand, if you're a student of literature, especially American literature, you may know her name as a poet yet never have realized that she's one of your kin in the grand family of faith.

### Anne Bradstreet's Background

I'm speaking of Anne Bradstreet. From a scriptural point of view, her biography could be summed up in the language of Paul: "Even though our outer nature is wasting away, our inner nature is being renewed day by day" (2 Cor. 4:16). Most biographies are external affairs: places, dates, events, people met, and circumstances encountered. This is fine. In fact, it's usually essential because we need the pegs of times and places on which to hang more important matters. But often that's all external data is good for—just pegs on which to hang the *real* story.

I admit a prejudice for internal biographies. I suspect this springs from another prejudice, my conviction that the most important events in our lives are those that affect our minds, our souls, and our spirits. That's why I keep pulling from my shelves Katherine Butler Hathaway's autobiography, *The Little Locksmith.* Very little was happening in her life through the years covered in her memoirs, but a great deal was unfolding in her inner being.

When it comes to Anne Bradstreet, there's also much to be said about the externals in her life, but the part that interests me most has to do with what went on in her soul.

According to the best historical estimates, Anne was born in 1612, probably at Northampton, in England. She grew up in a good, godly, and strict family. At age sixteen she married Simon Bradstreet, son of a Nonconformist minister. Such early marriages were not uncommon in those days, partly because life expectancy was short and partly because women were not often involved in an extended educational program. When Anne was eighteen, she and her husband immigrated across the Atlantic to the new land of America. This, as you can quickly calculate, was in 1630, just ten years after the landmark settlement at Plymouth Rock. The Bradstreets settled at first in what is now Cambridge, in the area of what is now Harvard Square, and then moved more permanently to what is now North Andover.

I recite all these details so easily, and you hear them in the same mood, because we instinctively "feel" travel in the context of modern air transportation, with temporary lodging in motels, after which we purchase a new home through a real estate agent, probably with the help of the Internet. But of course that isn't the kind of world Anne Bradstreet knew. The trip from England lasted from April 8 through June 12—more than nine weeks. When the ship finally landed on the shores of Massachusetts, many were sick of scurvy, the travel plague of the times, and many more became ill as they settled in the new world. A significant number were buried during the next few weeks. Food was scarce, so everyone lived on meager rations. The little colony was in constant peril for their lives. Only by the mercy of the Indians could their sickly number hope to survive. But survive they did. Both Anne's father, Thomas Dudley, and her husband, Simon, served as governors of the Massachusetts Bay Colony. Anne and Simon had eight children, four sons and four daughters, only one of whom died before Anne did. That may have been something of a record for those hard times. As for Anne's descendants, they are a notable lot.

They include William Ellery Channing, Richard H. Dana Jr., Wendell Phillips, and Oliver Wendell Holmes Sr., the writer, and his son, the Supreme Court Justice. If one puts together the literary and political achievements of these persons, along with their notable contributions to social reform, I venture that only the Adams family and the descendants of Jonathan Edwards deserve higher rank in our American story.

## Anne Bradstreet's Spiritual Story

But I've said that I'm interested in Anne Bradstreet for her interior story, and I've suggested that it's her role as our spiritual ancestor that especially matters. So what is it about her that makes her matter?

Anne's spiritual commitments began early. When she was only six or seven, as she recalled later, she "began to make conscience of [her] ways." That phrase rings quaint in our ears, doesn't it? And perhaps especially when we think of a six- or seven-year-old. I submit that while twenty-first–century six- and seven-year-olds might have little explicit sense of conscience, they usually have rather far-reaching knowledge of other matters. Young Anne used her conscience well. When she felt she had done something wrong, she was unable to rest "till by prayer I had confest it unto God." And she "found much comfort in reading the Scriptures."[1]

Most of us have observed, either in memories of our own childhood or in observing others, that children are often very sensitive to God and matters of faith and prayer. Robert Coles, professor of psychiatry and medical humanities at Harvard, makes that point in *The Spiritual Life of Children*. But puberty and the years immediately following are often a quite different matter. These can be years of spiritual wandering, sometimes with no full return to the faith commitments of childhood.

Anne went through such a period when she was fourteen or fifteen. As she put it, the "follies of youth" took hold of her. Our generation might wonder how that could be, since she didn't have drugs, television, or acid rock to lead her astray. I remind you that the devil has been alive and well all throughout history, The fact that his methodology now has electronic assistance doesn't really mean that evil is more powerful than it ever was.

I suspect Anne Bradstreet was much more spiritually sophisticated in her understanding of sin. She confessed that pride and vanity were her great problems. Believe me, that's dealing with basics. You and I are part of a time in which, both in and out of the church, we are quite superficial in our understanding of sin. Let us confess that *sin* is not a key word in our vocabulary. We've developed so many synonyms for the word that we're rarely required to use it in its unadorned form. When we do, we largely relegate it to the headline stuff of the publications at the super market checkout counter. We don't often face up to the profound and private places of our hearts. "Know thyself," ancient wisdom has advised. "Not if it will make me uncomfortable," we answer.

## Anne Bradstreet's Inner Struggles

Her inner struggles took a variety of forms. Moving to America with her husband was not easy. She loved her homeland, and it was difficult to face "a new world and new manners." How did she manage it? After she was "convinced it was the will of God," she "submitted to it." We can only guess how much struggle she endured before the submitting came, but submit she did. Her beliefs themselves were often tried. Satan troubled her, she said, "concerning the verity of the scriptures, many times by Atheisme how I could know there was a God." She sensed at times that her "love of the pleasant things of this life" might be unchristian. Still with it all, she grew in faith and character.

## Anne Bradstreet and Biblical Themes

As I noted earlier, Anne Bradstreet loved the Bible. It's easy to see that she was familiar with its language. Her journal, her poems, and her letters contain biblical quotations the way our letters are likely to refer to the news of the day. One way and another, it's clear that the biggest business of her life was to live in a way that would please God.

One of the feel-good religious themes of our time is that if we please God, everything will come up roses. It didn't always prove so for Miss Bradstreet. She went through several periods of sickness in a time when pain wasn't easily relieved. Through it all, she rejoiced in the goodness of God that sustained her. On a day in May, 1657, after a period of illness, she said that God had blessed her difficult period with many refreshings. Now, she said, "I chiefly labour for a contented, thankful heart. I hope," she continued, that "my soul shall flourish while my body decays, and the weakness of this outward man shall be a means to strengthen my inner man."[2]

She had read the apostle Paul, hadn't she? Her prayer is hardly other than an adaptation of Paul's words to her immediate experience. Perhaps it was her familiarity with scripture that caused her to interpret her experiences in such far-seeing fashion. You and I are naturally inclined to seek our personal benefit, particularly those benefits most immediately within reach. But the scriptures teach us to seek benefits that go far beyond ourselves, personal benefits that are more profound and more far-reaching both in this world and in the world to come.

I'm uneasy that sometimes, in my preaching and teaching, I seem to encourage spiritual growth as it relates to immediate benefits, sometimes even to material advantage. So much contemporary thinking seems to see spirituality as a means to physical, psychological, or economic benefits. For Anne Bradstreet, it was quite the opposite. She saw the physical and material issues of life as a possible means to spiritual development. I confess gladly that when we follow God, blessings are likely to follow us. Without a doubt, doing what is right is more likely to bring a variety of blessings into our lives—social, economic, and physical. However, we need to see these results as peripheral to our main pursuit which is our relationship to God, and to the ensuing quality of our life with others. Miss Bradstreet got the order right.

## Anne Bradstreet's Earthly Relationships

Not that she was so spiritually-minded as to be removed from this earth. The farthest thing from it! She was very much part of her world and lived it to the full. One of the best evidences is her relationship with her husband, Simon. One of her poems to him is often included in anthologies of love poetry. Hear these few lines:

If ever two were one, then surely we.
If ever man were lov'd by wife, then thee;
If ever wife was happy in a man,
Compare with me the women if you can.[3]

As I said earlier, her Simon became an important leader in the colony, including its governorship, which meant he was often gone from home for extended periods. On one such occasion she wrote,

If two be one, as surely thou and I,
How stayest thou there, whilst I at Ipswich lie?[4]

Perhaps the greatest test of Anne's life came on a night in July, 1666. She was awakened suddenly from her sleep by cries of "Fire!" Facilities for fighting fire were almost non-existent, so everything was quickly destroyed. The years of building a home and accumulating valuables, both economic and sentimental, were in one night—indeed, in a few hours—taken from her. In a poem apparently written only a few hours later, she looks at the ruins and recalls where things once were:

Here stood that trunk, and there that chest;
There lay that store I counted best...
All of it now, she said, "My pleasant things in ashes lie."

So how did she respond to such loss? At first, she says, she mourned that no guest would ever again sit under her roof or anyone eat again at the table. That response, of itself, seems to me to be a social, rather than a selfish, one. But she soon chides her heart:

Thou hast an house on high erect;
Framed by that mighty Architect...
And this house in the world to come is "purchased, and paid
    for, too, / By Him who hath enough to do."
Farewell, my pelf; farewell, my store;
The world, no longer let me love.
My hope and treasure lie above.[5]

That's good religion. It's also good sense, as good religion always is ultimately. When you've lost so much that in this world you hold dear, you do well if you can put it in perspective and know there is more to life than what you can lay your hands on. A materialist, now or ever, might say to Anne, "You've lost everything!" Anne might answer, "Not really. My Eternal Architect has laid out a home for me that is beyond the reach of fire or storm; yes, and beyond inflation or changing property values. It will be waiting for me when it's time for me to move in." In such a response, Anne would reflect the writer of the Epistle to the Hebrews, who said that people of faith "desire a better country, that is, a heavenly one. Therefore God is not ashamed to be called their God; indeed, he has prepared a city for them" (Heb. 11:16).

## Anne Bradstreet's Legacy

Anne Bradstreet was no embarrassment to God. She was quite a lady. She came to the crude shores of America when she was a teenage wife, survived sickness and deprivation, bore and raised eight children, and provided a loving home. In a world and a time when only men were expected to write poetry, she put her thoughts on paper, much to the bewilderment of some of her more conventional neighbors. We can be grateful that her brother-in-law, without Anne's knowing, took her poems to England where they were published and that eventually, six years after her death, an American edition was published. Thus she became one of the first poets to write English verse in the American colonies. Her complete works were published more than three centuries later in 1981. She has a unique place in American literature and, through her descendants, in American political and literary history.

But above all, she walked with God. Without a doubt, this is the way she would want to be remembered. Her life was not to be measured by the house in which she lived, which she lost to fire, Certainly her husband's success, which is remembered primarily today because of the woman to whom he was married, offered no standard for measuring her life. Even the poetry she wrote, lovely as it is, did not provide a standard for success. She had her sights set on the eternal. She recognized with Paul that "what can be seen is temporary, but what cannot be seen is eternal" (2 Cor. 4:18). She was wise enough to keep her vision clear and to govern all her decisions, large and small, by that standard.

She is a great, great spiritual ancestor. I introduce you to her proudly. As I do so, I challenge myself, as I challenge you, to live up to the pattern she so modestly set.

# CHAPTER 5

# Blaise Pascal
## *A Night of Transforming Passion*

### Introducing Blaise Pascal

Over the years I have quoted Pascal in a number of sermons and have used him in illustrative ways, especially his dramatic religious experience. I have never made him the sole theme of a sermon, but I still hope to do so. He is one of the true, full-blown geniuses of human history, with such a variety of skills and achievements that one finds his name not only in a general encyclopedia, but also in specialized volumes in science, philosophy, religion, mathematics, and literature. All of this though he lived barely 39 years!

Pascal holds particular interest to the preacher. His achievements in science and mathematics put him in exclusive company in these fields, but in his later years his Christian faith became more important to him than his scientific pursuits. Thus he is especially significant in our generation, where for so many, science is god.

### *Basic Background*

Pascal was born June 19, 1623, in Clermont-Ferrand, France. He died August 19, 1662, in Paris. He was educated at home by his father, who taught him primarily in ancient languages. His father refused to work with him in the sciences until he discovered that Blaise, then 12, had taught himself geometry. At the age of 16, Blaise got the attention of the great René Descartes by writing a book, *The Geometry of Conics*. Between the ages of 19 and 21, he invented a digital calculator.

Soon thereafter he perfected studies of pressure and liquid in what we now know as Pascal's Law. With Pierre de Fermat, he invented the theory of probability. In the field of literature, his *Provincial Letters*– a series of religious essays–is described as "the beginning of modern French prose." Of course, his *Pensées* is  still published in paperback and excerpts are included in all sorts of collections.

### Communities of Interest

Pascal's appeal cuts through a wide variety of intellectual communities. We can confess at the outset that many will say they've never heard of him. Yet each syringe pays tribute to him, as does each sophisticated gambling table (ironically!). Many have turned to "Pascal's Wager" in the course of their search for faith without knowing the wager's source.

Pascal appeals especially to two groups of persons who are not always easy for us to reach: the scientific/mathematical mind and the lover of fine literature. The first group is impressed by Pascal's genius in their fields, and the latter one by Pascal's mastery of French prose, as shown particularly in his *Pensées*.

Here's some special counsel to the preacher. If your scientific background is limited (as mine is), avoid getting into waters so deep as to embarrass yourself. On the other hand, if you have a fair amount of scientific training, avoid becoming so technical that you lose the interest of the average listener.

## SERMON _____

# Blaise Pascal: *A Night of Transforming Passion*

## Scripture Lesson: 2 Corinthians 12:1–5

Language is suffering inflation in our time. This is partly the fault of the advertising and public relations industries, which depend on such language for their very existence. I suspect this inflation is caused also by our hunger for heroes. If we can't come up with bona fide heroes, we will manufacture some by the process of exaggeration.

Take the word *genius*. Obviously, it's the sort of word that should be used sparingly. Use it too much, and it becomes meaningless. No matter! The word is now tossed about freely. Let a child finger her way through her first neighborhood piano recital, and some kind friend will call her "a budding genius." We may never see the flower.

The sports broadcaster, forced to deal almost entirely in superlatives, tells us that a certain wide receiver is a "genius at finding his way into the open seam," whatever that may mean. Even the literary critic, who seems to survive more on acid than on honey, is likely to say of a first novel, "Perhaps we have a new genius on our hands."

Well, it's time to remind ourselves that a genius, by definition, is someone with exceptional natural capacity–that is likely to appear early–and with particular gifts for creativity and originality. We should also remember that an order of nobility exists within the ranks of geniuses, so that not all geniuses are created equal.

## Blaise Pascal's Background

I say all of this by way of talking about a man who not only deserves the title "genius," but who is in the rare group of those at the very top of this classification. And more! His particular genius was in the areas of mathematics and science, but he was also a philosopher, a theologian, and a man of letters. He was a master of French prose. In his own time, he engaged in sophisticated theological debates and his insights are still quoted and argued today. If I may seem to contradict my own concern for the word genius, I would also praise this man as a genius in compassion and in breadth of human concern.

His name was Blaise Pascal. He was born in Clermont, France, on June 19, 1623, into a family of some economic and social substance. His father was a government official. When Blaise was eight, the family moved to Paris, then a little later to Rouen. They lived very comfortably, and Pascal's father associated not only with people who were economically and politically powerful but also with people who were leaders in science and the arts.

The elder Pascal was himself a fine scholar, so he insisted on educating his son at home. He concentrated almost exclusively on ancient languages, with no work in the sciences. He discovered, however, when Blaise was twelve, that the boy had already taught himself geometry. When Blaise was sixteen, he wrote a book, *The Geometry of Conics,* that got the attention of none other than René Descartes. As someone has said, Pascal's mind was active rather than accumulative. He thought for himself, discovering rather than being told.

## Blaise Pascal's Accomplishments

His restless mind insisted on opening new doors. Somewhere between the ages of nineteen and twenty-one, he invented a digital calculator. Not long after, he developed what is now known in physics as Pascal's Law, from which has come such developments as hydraulic presses, hydraulic elevators, vacuum pumps, and air compressors. Then, with Pierre de Fermat, he invented the theory of probability. Shortly before his death in 1662, he invented the omnibus, a horse-drawn wagon that provided Paris with the first public mass transportation system. This invention reflected the deep sense of social conscience that came to Pascal in his later years. He hoped to make transportation available to the poor, so people could move easily and inexpensively from one area to another. He directed that any profits which might come from the system would go to charitable purposes.

As for literature, no less a stylist than T. S. Eliot said that Pascal's prose was "of capital importance in the foundation of French classical style."[1] He perfected his style in his *Letters to a Provincial,* a series of eighteen "letters" in which he made his case for Jansenism, a body of doctrine within Roman Catholicism that was popular for a time but was vigorously opposed by the Jesuits. One of his insights on writing is good in any language. One might call it the first rule of composition. I think it also demonstrates Pascal's sense of humor: "I have made this [letter] longer than usual, only because I have not had the time to make it shorter." I wonder if preachers might sometimes explain their sermon length the same way!

## The Night of Transforming Passion

So Blaise Pascal was a genius in mathematics, in physics, in philosophy, in theology, and in literature; but in truth, I wouldn't be preaching about Pascal if it were only a matter of his accumulated and wide-ranging greatness. I bring him to you because he was a passionate believer in Jesus Christ, so much so that in the latter years of his life he felt that this was his only true significance.

On the other hand, I might not be telling you his story if all I could say of him had to do with his Christian passion. Vast numbers of persons—some well-known but most little-known—have possessed such passion. Not as many as I wish, let me hasten to say, but a larger number than we usually realize. No, I tell you Pascal's story because of this combination: he was a true genius in a variety of fields, a bona fide intellectual, who was also as thorough-going a Christian believer as you're likely to find. Many people, especially among the "cultured despisers of Christianity,"[2] think that no intellectual genius can also be a simple believer. Pascal demonstrates otherwise.

I want to tell you a good deal about his faith, but let me begin with his night of transforming passion. Pascal recorded what happened that night, though I'm not sure he recorded his experience for the benefit of others. His written memo may have been entirely for his own edification so that he might read it again and again, much the way some of us might pull out a particular snapshot because of the pleasure it gives us to see it again.[3]

The date was a Monday, November 23, 1654. The time was the two-hour period between 10:30 p.m. and 12:30 a.m. The defining word, as Pascal wrote it, was *FIRE*. From whence the fire? "God of Abraham, God of Isaac, God of Jacob, not of the philosophers and scholars." With that, Pascal noted two scripture passages, Exodus 3:6 and Matthew 22:32. Then Pascal wrote five words: "Certitude. Certitude. Feeling. Joy. Peace." I'm interested that he wrote "certitude" twice. This is a scientist, a scholar, a person who pursues truth until he feels as little doubt remains as is humanly possible. Having found such certainty, he says it twice: Certitude, Certitude.

From that certainty, Pascal wrote, "Forgetfulness of the world and of everything except God." A few lines later the scientist added simply, "Joy, joy, joy, tears of joy." Then, a few lines farther, he quoted John 17:3: "This is the eternal life, that they might know Thee, the only true God, and the one whom Thou has sent, Jesus Christ" (English translation of Pascal's French writing) Then as if he found the words sweet to his tongue, Pascal said once, then again, "Jesus Christ. Jesus Christ." He promised that he would keep himself in "total submission" to Jesus Christ and to his director, the priest who was his spiritual mentor.

Clearly, this was an ecstatic religious experience. But it was not a "free-standing experience." It was set within the context of the scriptures and the Church. Thus at the outset Pascal identifies the time not simply by the calendar date, but also by the feast days of the Catholic Church. As for the scriptures, Pascal includes eight biblical references. He placed all that he experienced under the discipline of scripture and tradition. He had no intention of starting something new. Indeed, he verified his experience by the fact that it came within the boundaries of the faith as he knew it. This scholar whose mind was always searching new areas of discovery wanted only to know God as God has been revealed through "the faith that was once for all entrusted to the saints" (Jude 1:3).

The experience of that night was so significant to Blaise Pascal that he not only wrote it down–trying as best he could to capture on paper that which was quite beyond capturing–but he sewed it into the lining of his jacket. Obviously, he meant to have it against his very person, next to his heart, in all his comings and goings. A servant found it there after Pascal's death, nearly ten years later.

## Blaise Pascal's Wager of Faith

What shall we make of this experience? Let's begin by reminding ourselves of the kind of person Pascal was. I think of a classic line from his *Pensées:* "Man is only a reed, the most feeble thing in nature; but he is a thinking reed."[4] "All our dignity," Pascal continues, "consists in thought." This is a person who holds reason in reverence. He doesn't see us humans as simply a bundle of emotions or as helpless victims of circumstances. Fragile as we are, we have the ability to think, and that makes all the difference.

Pascal's commitment to reason carried over into his faith pilgrimage. He would not allow his faith to be a sentimental thing from which he shut out reason. This man who developed the theory of probability brought the issue of his belief in God to just such logical ground. Listen: "'God is, or God is not.' But to which side shall we incline?" Pascal admits that according to reason, we can defend neither proposition. But he insists that we "must wager. It is not optional." We can't go through life saying we won't decide, because we have to decide. To put it in our modern setting, there's a coin flip to start this game. It's going to happen whether or not we choose between heads and tails. So what shall we choose? Pascal, in what has come to be known as "Pascal's Wager," reasons, "Let us weigh the gain and the loss in wagering that God is. Let us estimate these two chances. If you gain, you gain all. If you lose, you lose nothing. Wager, then, without hesitation, that He is."[5]

Some of life's decisions can be postponed. Indeed, they can be postponed even until death. As a scientist, Pascal didn't complete all of his experiments. In one sense, some of his experiments are being completed even to this very day. But in the matter of Pascal's own soul, only he could finish the experiment of personal faith. He was compelled, therefore, to make his choice, to commit himself to a wager. So he chose to bet on God. As a student of probability, he saw it as the simplest judgment: either God is or God is not. If God is and I have wagered on him, I gain all. If God is not and I have wagered on him, I have lost nothing. So then, why hesitate? Wager on God!

Well, Pascal did place that wager. On that November night some three and a half centuries ago, his wager consummated in two hours of joy—not joy of the philosophers and scholars of whom he was one, but the joy of the people of faith, of Abraham, Isaac, and Jacob—of whom, also, Pascal was one.

## Blaise Pascal's Quest for God

But this night did not stand alone. It didn't come, so to speak, out of the blue. It was the product of Pascal's lifelong quest for God. Life at its best is a pilgrimage that leads to God and, if there is time enough, a pilgrimage onward within the purposes of God. Some of us find more details within this pilgrimage than do others, but the details are inevitably there.

In Blaise Pascal's case, the story begins with a father who was himself a devout man and a true seeker after God. Then came the influence of the Deschamps brothers, two men who had been famous throughout Normandy for their violence, but who were wonderfully converted and became witnesses of mercy and devotion. While caring for Blaise's father after he suffered a dislocated hip, the two men paid particular attention to Blaise himself. These conversations played a key part in the family becoming part of the Jansenist movement.

I won't try to explain the teachings of Jansenism, even though they were so important to Pascal. It would take too long to make such an explanation, and I'm afraid that I might easily leave you confused. Instead, let me refer to T. S. Eliot, who said that Pascal was no doubt "attracted as much by the fruits of Jansenism...as by the doctrine itself."

The Christianity being practiced at the time in France was "relaxed and easy-going," without much sense of its intended depth and integrity. So Pascal, a person of passion and commitment, was drawn to the Jansenists who were devout, ascetic, and truly heroic in the practice of the Catholic faith.[6] Sometimes we are influenced not so much by the specifics of a doctrine as by the quality of life it produces. Add to all this the fact that Pascal was a faithful student of the Bible and knew the scriptures well. Remember he faithfully sought God daily, both through the services of the church and through his private devotions.

## Blaise Pascal's Legacy

With all of this discipline, Pascal's walk with God was marked by great joy. His sister Jacqueline was sometimes troubled that her brother was "so jolly a penitent."[7] With the passage of time he also became deeply concerned for the poor—a special aspect of conversion, it seems to me, for someone who has always known financial comfort and who may find it hard to grasp the problems of those who have not.

The last two years of Pascal's life were lived in constant physical distress; it may have been meningitis, cancer of the spine, or a malignant stomach ulcer. During that period he wrote a prayer "Asking God to use illness to a good end." "Thou hadst given me health that I might serve Thee, and I have profaned it," he prayed. Then, reflecting the Calvinism of Jansenism, he spoke of his illness as sent from God to correct his ways, and continued, "I have misused my health, and Thou hast justly punished me for it; do not suffer me to misuse Thy punishment."[8]

Pascal died early in the morning of August 19, 1662, only two months after his thirty-ninth birthday. He was a genius, no doubt of that. But I cherish his memory because of his transparent goodness and his passionate love of God. He makes a good patron saint for all those who want to think, but who want also to believe; and who want to believe with passion and total commitment.

# CHAPTER 6

# Johann Sebastian Bach
*Happy Birthday, Brother Bach!*

### Introducing Bach

I preached this sermon during the year the world was celebrating the 300th anniversary of Bach's birth. I'm not exaggerating when I say "the world was celebrating," because events honoring Bach were mounted in literally every part of the world. This meant that resource material was abundantly available. I preached the same sermon several years later, on the 250th anniversary of Bach's death, using the same title, but changing the conclusion with an explanation that, for a person of Bach's faith, the day of death is the day of wondrous birth into the world to come.

This sermon was well-received not only by my own congregation, but also by our radio audience, since the radio station (WCLV) on which my sermons were broadcast each Sunday morning was known as the Cleveland Orchestra station and thus had a base audience of music lovers. In choosing biographical themes, keep such particularities in mind and ask whether the community finds its pride in sports, country music, literature, or politics.

*Basic Background*

Johann Sebastian Bach was born in Eisenbach, Germany, March 21, 1685. His parents died before he was ten, so his older brother raised him. The brother taught him the clavichord and harpsichord. Bach married his cousin Maria in 1707, and they had seven children before her death in 1720. A year later he married a professional singer, Anna Magdalena Wilcken, with whom he had thirteen children.

They moved to Leipzig in 1723, where Bach spent the rest of his life. His latter years he was nearly blind. He died of a stroke in 1750. It's interesting to note that his choirs were usually only twelve voices, so that his emphasis was on spiritual quality rather than physical size. Two of Bach's sons, C. P. E. and Johann Christian, also became fine musicians and composers.

### Communities of Interest

Obviously Bach's greatest appeal is to musicians and lovers of fine music. But it's surprising how widespread that interest is. Many people will identify themselves apologetically as liking Bach but "not really able to appreciate him." His story speaks especially to persons of Germanic heritage. While Lutherans lay special claim to Bach, all Protestant and Catholic bodies relate to him. Bach's son, Johann Christian, converted to the Roman Catholic Church and composed much music for their purposes. Bach's appeal in Japan, where only one per cent of the population is Christian, has opened the door for much missionary work there.

## SERMON _____

# Johann Sebastian Bach:
## *Happy Birthday, Brother Bach!*

## Scripture Lesson: Psalm 150

### Johann Sebastian Bach's Background

Now and then our human race is blessed by the appearance of a true and absolute genius. The names of these landmark personalities tower over not only the mass of humanity, but also the otherwise "great" figures of human history, making even great persons seem ordinary by comparison. I wouldn't be so audacious as to venture a complete list, but one thinks immediately of Pascal, Michelangelo, Leonardo da Vinci, Shakespeare, Albert Einstein, and Bach: *Johann Sebastian Bach.*

I dare to suggest that Bach may have extended more blessing and more pleasure to the human race than anyone else in the notable group I've just listed. It was his privilege to work with the medium of music, and music has several advantages. For one, it is more easily transported from one place to another than, say, painting or sculpture. Because music needs no translation, as does literature, or no interpretation, as does science or mathematics, its passage from one nation, language, or culture to another is much simpler and more direct.

Early in my pastoral ministry, I used to think of Bach often on Saturday mornings. I would be in my church study, concluding the writing of my sermon. In the sanctuary below, the church organist would be rehearsing the prelude, postlude, and offertory for the Sunday services. On those occasions when my sermonizing hit a snag, I'd envy the organist. She didn't have to compose her work for the next day, as I was doing. She needed only to master what someone else had composed. Then I'd think of Johann Sebastian Bach.

## Bach's Achievements

During his first several years as cantor at St. Thomas Church in Leipzig, Bach wrote a cantata for nearly every Sunday and every church holiday. Mind you, being the organist at St. Thomas wasn't his only responsibility. He was expected to oversee the music program in three other churches in Leipzig, as well as teach music and Latin during the week at the Saint Thomas School!

All told, Bach wrote nearly 300 cantatas, some 200 of which are available today on recording. This is to say, they were *good,* so good they are enduring classics. He produced masterworks week after week, between teaching classes in Latin, working with private students, administering music programs, and wrangling with his employers, who often seemed dull to Bach's genius. When we add his compositions for organ, violin, cello, flute, trumpet, harpsichord, voice, choir, orchestra—in sonatas, suites, cantatas, oratorios, masses, motets, and concertos—we have an accumulation of over a thousand works, and all of them of enduring quality.

While multitudes pay Bach the tribute of listening to his work or seeking out recordings of his compositions, his most eloquent tributes come from his fellow musicians. Indeed, the greater the musician, the higher the tribute. Bach was virtually forgotten when Beethoven performed his *Saint Matthew Passion* exactly a century after Bach himself first performed it. Beethoven's performance restored Bach to the world. Beethoven, an almost incomparable genius in his own right, described Bach as an ocean of creativity compared to whom all other composers were mere brooks.[1]

Pablo Casals, the premier cellist of his generation and an honored composer, said that "Bach, like nature [is] a miracle."[2] Ernest Bloch, one of the finest composers of the twentieth century, often told his classes at Berkeley, "Whenever I have a question, I always ask Mr. Bach. And he always has the answer."[3] Someone asked biologist Lewis Thomas what message he thought we should send to other possible civilizations in space in a rocket we fired with some of the best of earth in its cone. Thomas answered, "I would send the complete works of Johann Sebastian Bach." Then, after a pause, he added, "But that would be boasting."[4]

## Bach as the Fifth Evangelist

Perhaps by chance what I'm saying doesn't impress you. Maybe you think Bach is high brow, and you never listen to him. Let me insist that you don't have to go to church or to classical musical programs to hear Bach's works. I think, for instance, of television commercials a few years ago that sought to sell us computers, by way of Bach's music in the background. Probably only a very competent music student can estimate how often Bach's compositions–especially his *Tocatta* and his *Fugue in D Minor*–have been used as background music in movies.

Nevertheless, if Bach were simply a great man, a magnificent composer, and yes, a genius, I wouldn't preach a sermon about him. It's not that I don't have regard for human achievement. I'm impressed that the whole world is celebrating Mr. Bach's 300th birthday this year [1985], with special events in his honor in a constellation that includes Boston, Dallas, Dublin, Krakow, Vienna, and Tokyo, but I wouldn't preach about someone for that reason.

I see the pulpit as a sacred forum. I will discuss a wide variety of subjects from the pulpit and will illustrate my thinking from secular as well as sacred vantage points, but I work with the conviction that everything I say in the pulpit must come under the Lordship of Jesus Christ. My themes must ultimately and surely point to God and to the kind of intellectual, spiritual,  economic, and political life God might expect us to live.

Why, then, J. S. Bach? My thinking could be summarized by the title often given to Mr. Bach–"the Fifth Evangelist." Those who use this term aren't thinking of Billy Graham and Billy Sunday, but the classical use of the word *Evangelist,* as a reference to the four gospels. So we have Matthew, Mark, Luke, and John–and Johann Sebastian Bach. Now of course I don't really mean to put Mr. Bach at the same level as the New Testament scriptures, nor do those who have described him with this phrase. It's simply a way of saying that Bach was a great and virtually unique communicator of the gospel of Jesus

Christ. Roger Fry, the sometimes acidic English art critic of the early twentieth century, once said, "Bach almost persuades me to be a Christian."[5] Evangelist, indeed!

## Bach's Personal Faith

Bach's profound personal faith was not by accident. He was the son of not only the most famous musical family of his time, but also a family of devoted Christians. His ancestors had left Hungary during the Thirty Years War rather than give up their faith. Bach continued in that commitment. I have never come upon a specific story of Bach's religious conversion. Perhaps in such a family, he accepted the faith in pieces, as he grew up, until at last it possessed him. Or perhaps some of the very great trials through which he passed became the womb that gave birth to his great faith.

In any event, the evidence of his faith is all around us. He was a student of the Bible. His well-marked Bible, residing in Concordia Seminary in St. Louis, is proof of that. He not only underlined passages the way many of us underline a book that captures us but also wrote in the margins his personal responses, prayers, and insights in the language of a true Christian pilgrim. He was, as someone has said, "a Christian who lived with the Bible."

He was raised as an orthodox Lutheran, so we're probably not surprised that his personal library included two sets of the writings of Martin Luther. His library also contained many of the German pietistic works. I suspect these readings added a unique quality of warmth and personal passion to his musical interpretation.

## Genius Devoted to Jesus

Somewhere along the way, Bach made a profound dedication of his grand, enormous talent to God and to Jesus Christ. Often his manuscripts bear the letters *JJ,* an abbreviation for the Latin, *Jesu juva*–"Jesus, help me." Here was the cry of an artist who realized that the gift within him could not find its best expression unless he received help from his Lord and Savior. William Buckley says that Bach's achievements cannot be explained short of a belief in God.[6] His native talent was great, a divine gift indeed, but Bach was devout enough to know that talent was not enough. He sensed his need for the touch of God upon his work, and we can only conclude that he received it, and received it in extravagant abundance.

Bach never forgot from whence his genius came. The inscription that most often accompanied his compositions was *SDG,* for the Latin, *Soli Deo Gloria:* "To the glory of God alone." He went about all of his composing in this mood. A predominate share of his work was done for the church. He also wrote a fair amount of secular music, and the secular as well as the sacred was likely to be noted with the same, "*Soli Deo Gloria.*"

Richard Dinwiddie tells of a time when he asked a class in church music to listen to a Bach cantata (in German). Then he asked for their reactions. They were so accustomed to Bach's "church sound" that they made several sincere comments regarding the spiritual blessing the music had given them. Only then did Dinwiddie reveal that the music was Bach's cantata extolling the delights of drinking coffee![7]

Perhaps then Bach wouldn't be upset to hear his music performed as part of a television commercial, provided, of course, he could find justifying beauty in the given product. In any event, the esteemed twentieth-century composer, Leonard Bernstein, got it right when he wrote in his book, *Joy of Music,* "For Bach, all music was religion; writing it was an act of faith; and performing it was an act of worship. Every note was dedicated to God and nothing else."[8]

## Bach the Teacher

Bach taught his students to dedicate their work to God in the same fashion. In his rules and principles of accompaniment, he explained how they should use the figured-bass in their playing. He said that if rightly done,, the result would be "an agreeable harmony to the glory of God and justifiable gratification of the senses; for the sole end of general-bass, like that of all music, should be nothing else than God's glory and pleasant recreation." Then he added a sentence that might seem to some of us to be a prophecy about some of what is called music today: "Where this object is not kept in view, there can be no true music, but an infernal scraping and bawling."[9]

## Bach the Unrecognized Genius

I mentioned earlier that Bach almost always dedicated his compositions "to the glory of God alone." If you have an ironic sense of humor, you will conclude that in his own lifetime, Bach's prayer was answered. His genius as a composer was never widely recognized until nearly two generations after his death. He spent over twenty-five years as cantor and music director at St. Thomas Church in Leipzig, but the people never realized what they had. He was their third choice when he was hired. When he came to the post, one town councilor said, "If we can't have the best, we must make do with what there is." Near the end of his career, his sight began to fail, and his health in general was weakened. A year before he died, the Leipzig Council was already openly looking for his successor.

After his death, the sons of his first marriage (he had seven children by his first wife and thirteen by his second, ten of whom survived to adult life) argued with the sons of the second marriage over his estate. His compositions were sold at a fraction of their value, and some were lost. Some say that some of those compositions were even used to wrap garbage.

Some ninety obituaries were written at the time of his death, an admirable tribute, but only three mentioned him as a composer. He was appreciated by his own generation almost exclusively for his skills at the organ and harpsichord. "To the glory of God alone." It surely turned out that way.

## Bach in Modern View

If Bach's own generation saw him as a performer rather than as a composer, ours is as badly in error in another way. A majority of those who currently appreciate Bach's genius as a composer seem almost oblivious to the faith that inspired his genius. Thus, when *Newsweek* magazine did a cover story on Bach (December 24, 1984), its writers made no reference to his Christian commitments. I doubt that this was intentional or malicious. I suspect it's only that those involved in the story, and their editors, simply weren't equipped to understand this quality in the man. They were blind men trying to describe the colors on a da Vinci canvas. Johann Sebastian Bach was a genius, no doubt about it. More than that, he was a God-possessed, Christ-dedicated craftsman, who saw his talent as a gift from God which he must, therefore, return to God.

## Bach's Legacy

Sometimes a sermon is preached from the specific words of a scripture lesson, and sometimes from the unfolding of a story. I followed a different path this morning. I chose a scripture passage that I felt simply encompassed the spirit and indeed the essence of all I had to say, Psalm 150. This Psalm concludes the entire book of Psalms. It urges us humans, in a wonderfully exuberant way, to praise God with every instrument at our disposal: trumpet, harp, lyre, tambourine, strings, flute, and cymbals. That's what Johann Sebastian Bach did. He wrote music for every imaginable instrument, including the human voice, so we humans might praise God with a multitude of sounds.

And this grand Psalm concludes, "Let everything that breathes praise the LORD!" (Ps. 150:6). That's what Mr. Bach did. He praised the Lord as long as he had breath. When he died, on July 28, 1750, after a second stroke, he was dictating a chorale he was never able to finish. The chorale was entitled, "Before Thy Throne I Now Approach." He interrupted his composition to make the journey and fulfill the deed. Perhaps I speak sentimentally, but let me suggest that having no more breath with which to praise God on this earth, Bach took a full draught of new, divine air and finished his song on the other side.

We can only guess what goes on in heaven. Since everyone has the same credentials for guessing, I'll offer an idea just now. I wonder if perhaps Dr. Bach is even now composing music for the heavenly choirs. After all, why shouldn't the talents that heaven gave him continue to be employed in heaven? Some day, please God, you and I can check it out for ourselves.

CHAPTER 7

# Ancestors We'd Rather Forget
## *The Salem Witch Trial*

### Introducing the Salem Witch Hunt and Hypocrisy

No charge against the church is raised more frequently and more hurtfully than that we nurture hypocrites. In its own way, this accusation is a tacit compliment. It acknowledges that the Christian life is such a worthy goal that people want to lay claim to it even though they don't intend to live it. But the compliment is lost in the pain of the accusation. Most of us also recognize that those who seek excellence in any field thereby become a target for those who try to feel better about themselves by bringing someone else down. This is true for athletes ("With the money she makes, she should be able to return that serve"), for physicians ("How can he talk to me about health, with his avoirdupois?"), and for scholars ("If she's so smart, why can't she balance a checkbook?").

But especially, people like to attack those who fall short in living out their religious profession. Such failures appeal to the worst in us because all of us know we should be better than we are. If someone who seems to make more of religion than we do, has demonstrable shortcomings, our failures don't seem so bad.

Nevertheless, the hard and painful fact is this: we church folk aren't a perfect lot. No one knows that better than those of us who have served time as parish pastors. I happily declare that in my thirty-eight years in the pastorate I knew an extraordinary number of saints. But I surely had my share of people whose profession of faith embarrassed me. I sometimes took sorry consolation in the fact that I might well have embarrassed them, too. But that kind of reasoning never relieved me of the sad feeling that the church ought to be better than it is. We are sometimes criticized unfairly, but in many instances we fall inexcusably short of the name we bear.

So several years ago, I faced the matter squarely by choosing to deal with one of the most painful scenes from American church history: the Salem witch hunt of the late seventeenth century. While telling the story of one man, Samuel Parris, perhaps the key figure in the incident, I was able to deal obliquely with Christian shortcomings in general and with issues of distorted history and of forgotten details.

I preached this sermon in a church that was proud of its historic congregational roots. It's a theme that deserves a hearing, partly as an attempt to keep history in balance, partly as public confession, and partly to deal with the hard facts that we Christians have ancestors (and contemporaries) that we'd rather forget.

## Basic Background

In 1692 several young girls in Salem (Massachusetts), influenced by voodoo tales and the use of a crystal ball, became agitated to a point where the leaders of the community felt witches were at work. The new pastor, Samuel Parris, heightened the fears when he declared, "In this very church, God knows how many devils there are."[1] In time, nineteen persons were hanged as witches, and one was pressed to death. The incident has given a phrase to our common speech, "witch hunt." Persons judged to be witches had been executed earlier in the colonies, as they had in Europe. However, the extent of the Salem hysteria raised public conscience so that witches were never again executed in New England.

## Communities of Interest

This subject appeals to a wide and disparate group; those who love American history in general, New England history, our Puritan heritage, or social and intellectual history will respond to this story. So will persons who are fascinated by mass psychology and by the power of social movements. Even persons who aren't otherwise interested in church might respond to this theme.

# Samuel Parris:
## *One of the Ancestors We'd Rather Forget*

### Scripture Lesson: Psalm 41

According to an old saying, if any of us will look long enough at our family tree, we'll find some ancestor hanging from one of its branches. If that's true of our genealogical tree, I suspect it is truer still of the tree that represents our church family. The Christian church is proud of its saints, and believe me, we have many of them. That's why there's a place on the calendar for All Saints Day, because the church has long recognized that we have more saints than have ever been canonized. But we also have some people who seem to discredit the church. I want to talk with you today, as candidly and as fairly as possible, about one such person. I do so because he's part of our faith family tree. Rather than denying this fact or acting as if he didn't exist, we need to come to know him and to acknowledge him as part of our family.

### Samuel Parris and the Witch Trial Background

His name was Samuel Parris. Church history, including American church history, has its share of embarrassing chapters. Among the most painful is the chapter in which the Reverend Mr. Parris played a leading role. He didn't hold the stage alone, mind you, but he was probably the essence of its infamy.

It's possible you've never heard of him, and as I begin his story, it's likely you'd just as soon not hear of him now. If you recognize his name, it's probably because you've seen Arthur Miller's classic drama *The Crucible.* Samuel Parris was the minister in the community of Salem Farms at the time of the notorious Salem witchcraft trials. If any single figure stands out in that sorry story, it is probably Samuel Parris.

The story began in the winter of 1691–1692. You get a feel for the times if you remember that we date Plymouth Rock at 1620 and if I tell you that Salem was settled in 1626, which makes it one of America's oldest settlements. The winter of 1691–1692 a number of young women, including the Reverend Mr. Parris's daughter and niece, began meeting secretly in the Parris home. Tituba, a Barbados slave girl in the home, joined the girls in playing fortune telling. Then she began sharing some East Indian lore with the girls. Soon the girls, feeling guilty and confused, began behaving strangely. As their conduct grew more bizarre, their elders concluded they were victims of witchcraft.

The girls' parents believed the girls' stories, and began looking for the witches. The girls cooperated, often in hysterical fashion. At first, people singled out a number of social misfits, the kind of poor folks that we would judge today to be mentally ill or socially inept. Since their conduct was already peculiar, it was easy to put on them the dreadful "witch" label.

## Samuel Parris's Sermon

Samuel Parris then made matters dramatically worse. In a New England community in 1692 there was no more powerful position than the village pulpit. After all, the people had no radio or television and few, if any, periodicals. The pulpit was essentially the only source of authoritative information. Parris chose one Sunday to say, "In this very church, God knows how many devils there are."[2]

I suspect most of us pastors have had dark hours when we would have liked to say something like that, but most of us have risen above such momentary feelings! Not only did Parris say it, but he said it at the worst possible time.

## Controversy Aflame

The flame of controversy quickly began to spread. People began accusing their neighbors of ill-doing. Especially, accusations began to be levied against a number of middle-aged women. Then, members of some of the powerful families in the community who had opposed Parris's ministry came under fire. A large number belonged in this category, because Parris had been elected minister by a quite divided vote. Before the matter was done, over 150 suspects were imprisoned. Nineteen were hanged. The damage to the community was almost inconceivable.

In fact, the damage carries on to this very day. Salem—a name which, ironically, means *peace* as in *shalom*—is remembered more for this trial than for anything else in its very long history. We have a phrase in our common speech which almost surely is a product of the Salem event: when someone is being pursued in apparently unfair fashion by either the courts, by the press, or by simple, common gossip, we speak of it being a "witch hunt." So what happened in a tiny New England village more than three hundred years ago is with us still today.

At the heart of it all was this Congregational pastor, Samuel Parris. Who wants him as a spiritual ancestor–or for that matter, as any kind of ancestor? The playwright, Arthur Miller, wrote in his explanatory notes that Parris "cut a villainous path" in history, and that "there is very little good to be said for him."[3] The late Perry Miller, who perhaps knew more about the Pilgrims than anyone and who tried to be fair in his scholarship, said of Parris that he "appears utterly contemptible."[4]

So I repeat, who wants Samuel Parris? Someone will answer that we have him, whether we want him or not, but that we'd just as soon no one mentioned it. Someone else will say that he belonged to quite another, benighted age, so let's forget about him and move on.

Well, we should be careful about what we call "a benighted age," especially since we live in a time when most major newspapers carry an astrology column daily, and when the publications at the grocery checkout counter make embarrassing revelations of our contemporary taste. Sometime when you feel up to it, spend five minutes watching a popular morning or afternoon television show where people parade their pathologies and the studio audience responds in kind. You may begin to think that a few hundred people in a witch hunt can't compare with the fare in which contemporary millions invest their time.

## The Church and Samuel Parris

Back to Samuel Parris. A majority of his church members supported him, so he tried to remain as pastor after the Governor's order ended the trials. Parris confessed from his pulpit that he had been wrong. "God has been righteously spitting in my face," he said in graphic remorse. A council of leading, fellow clergy (some of whom were now reformed witch-hunters) recommended that, though Parris had done nothing wrong, he should leave his post. Nevertheless, Parris stayed on another year. At last he gave up the struggle and resigned his Salem Farms pulpit in July, 1696. Then, as Robert Booth has put it, he became "a scapegoat for the collective guilt of the colony."[5] I think I would be fair if I were to say that Parris himself became the victim of a new kind of witch hunt. He preached for a while at Stow, then took up farming and shop keeping in rural communities. He married again, had a new family, and became a schoolmaster. In time, he was permitted to become a supply minister, filling in where he was needed. In his old age he rode out to tiny villages to preach the gospel on Sunday mornings. When he died in 1720, at the age of 67, he wrote in his will that he was hopeful of "mercy from the Lord."[6]

## Modern Witch Trials and Their Victims

For our scripture reading this morning we chose Psalm 41. Let me remind you of some of those verses:

As for me, I said, "O LORD, be gracious to me;
  heal me, for I have sinned against you."
My enemies wonder in malice
  when I will die, and my name perish. (Ps. 41:4–5)
All who hate me whisper together about me;
  they imagine the worst for me. (Ps. 41:7)
Even my bosom friend in whom I trusted,
  who ate of my bread, has lifted the heel against me. (Ps. 41: 9)

That ancient prayer reminds us that we humans are so very fallible and that we live in a fallible world. Someone is always picking on someone else. Sometimes we are victimized by those we thought were our friends. As the psalmist said, "those who eat of our bread lift up the heel against us." Political associates of one year become adversaries the next. Siblings are torn apart when a will is probated. Church members, who have sung together, prayed together, and partaken of Holy Communion side by side become estranged over an issue, often a small one at that.

Our witch trials still go on, at personal levels. We are severed from one another by what our ancestors might have called demonic activity but which we describe by such words as "irrational behavior." "I don't see how a reasonable human being could do such a thing," we say. We don't hang those who upset us (though in our worst private moments we might wish we could), but in some instances the personal result is the same. For all practical purposes that person ceases to exist, except for moments in our rancorous thoughts.

## Motivating Factors Then and Now

Samuel Parris's story also reminds us that there's more to a person—and more to an event—than headlines and one-paragraph summaries. If I had known Samuel Parris in 1692, I'm not sure I would have liked him, but if I had been in Salem at the time, I don't know how I would have responded to what we now call the witchcraft hysteria. After all, the witch charges didn't begin with Parris. The physician who examined the distraught girls first labeled them as "bewitched." Parris followed the best "scientific" counsel available to him when he picked up the theme.

The community was at the time particularly susceptible to suggestions of supernatural evil. Because of the devastation of the Second Indian War, many New England settlers believed they were living "in the devil's snare." It is nearly impossible for us to move far enough into the mood of 1692 to understand the forces that were at work in Salem at that time.

## Samuel Parris in Historical Perspective

It's clear enough that Samuel Parris was not a perfect man. Having been chosen by such a small margin, he was unsure of his position. He knew that many of his parishioners didn't like him, and he didn't know how to cope with that fact. Besides, Salem Farms had been torn by petty feuds and nasty differences for many years. No doubt these feuds had contributed to the split vote on Parris's own candidacy. Parris didn't handle these matters well, and it appears he found it easy to think the worst–even witchery!–of those who disagreed with him. It's interesting, isn't it, that we speak today of "demonizing" our opponents? Samuel Parris may have led the way, but he wasn't the last.

Whatever his shortcomings, he was a human being and, in some respects, an admirable one. He repented of the wrong he had done and made public apology. He tried to rebuild his life after his grievous failure but was never allowed to do so. He spent the last, long third of his life in a measure of disgrace, trying to serve as a schoolmaster and as a supply clergy, always knowing he had done serious harm and constantly feeling that God had, indeed, righteously spat in his face. I'm impressed that in this he did not blame God, but accepted what he felt to be God's judgment.

Above all, I commend Samuel Parris for his willingness to repent. Alexander Pope said that "to err is human, to forgive divine." The link between that humanity and that divinity is repentance, the willingness to confess that an error has been made. This capacity to repent is a wondrous gift, but we humans are slow to exercise it. Parris had the character to do so.

"Ah," someone answers, "and he had plenty to repent of!" So he did, and so do we all. The extent of his error is not the question, because errors and sins, like beauty, are in the eye of the beholder. I wish only to make a case for his readiness to repent and to whatever degree possible, to make things right.

Again, a certain kind of pragmatist will say, "But it didn't do him any good, did it? He was never able to regain his place of prominence."

If the measure of a person's life is his or her position of prominence, then repenting did Parris little good. He continued through the long remaining days a man broken in career and public standing.

But whatever his faults, Parris knew that public opinion was not (and still is not) the ultimate judge. Parris wanted to be right with God and with his own conscience. He hoped still to have "mercy from the Lord," and he knew that the way to mercy is the road of repentance.

Samuel Parris is not one of our best ancestors, but I will confess that he is one of my spiritual kin. Let those who have never misjudged another person scorn him. Let those who have never used their power mischievously, destructively, or erratically pick up the first stone.

In my own final opinion, I know Samuel Parris was a badly flawed human being. I'm glad he cast himself upon the grace of our Lord Christ, confessed his shame, and tried during the remainder of his days to serve his fellows as best he could as school master and substitute pastor. If I understand the Christian gospel rightly, I expect that you and I will meet Samuel Parris in heaven. Provided, of course, that we have the grace, as he did, to repent of whatever our sins may be.

CHAPTER 8

# Samuel Johnson
## *A Man of His Word*

### Introducing Samuel Johnson

Few people have more citations in the various books of quotations
than Samuel Johnson. Some authorities say that Johnson ranks second
only to Shakespeare. The first great lexicographer, often described
as the greatest English writer of his century, Johnson preferred talk to
writing, even though he wrote with such exquisite skill. He may well
have been as delightful a conversationalist as our world has seen. But
this very gift, and his natural conviviality, probably limited Johnson's
literary output.

Everything I have just mentioned is fairly well known to anyone
who has a feeling for English literature. What we don't often hear
about Samuel Johnson is that he was a person of extraordinary
Christian devotion. He was a man whose generous spirit blessed all
who knew him, from servants to scholars, and whose written prayers
exude true piety.

### Basic Background

Samuel Johnson was born in Lichfield, England, in 1709, the son
of a bookseller. He attended Oxford University, 1728–1729, but had
to leave when he had exhausted his funds. His literary powers won
him early attention. In 1738 his satire, *London* was printed, followed
by a biography of Richard Savage. Then came *The Vanity of Human
Wishes* (1749). His monumental *Dictionary of the English Language*
occupied most of his writing time from 1747 to 1755.

He further established his ability as a scholar by his preface to his edition of Shakespeare's plays (1765) and by his critical essays, *The Lives of the English Poets.* James Boswell, Johnson's frequent companion, has established Johnson's gifts as a conversationalist, recording any number of Johnson's witty, incisive, challenging sentences in his two-volume biography, *The Life of Samuel Johnson, LL.D.*[1] Johnson died in 1784. Probably the best summary of Johnson's literary stature is demonstrated in the fact that critics speak of that period in English literature as "the Age of Johnson."

## Communities of Interest

Samuel Johnson's special appeal is to those persons who love literature or who love words. Students of eighteenth century literature (a select number, to be sure) are a made-to-order audience, but they will compel you to be sure of your data. If Johnson's prayers were more widely known, the persons who are drawn to retreats and to spiritual life weekends would want to know more about Johnson.

You might tell his story on the second Sunday of September when schools are resuming full operation (although the opening date now comes much earlier in most communities, it isn't felt emotionally until after Labor Day). You could also preach on Johnson when a sermon on learning is particularly appropriate. His story also can be appealing for certain special groups or events either within the congregation or in the community.

## SERMON

# Samuel Johnson: *A Man of His Word*

## Scripture Lesson: Psalm 119:9–16

I think I have always been reasonably appreciative of my teachers, even if in my teenage years I kept that appreciation rather well hidden. But my sense of appreciation seems now to increase every year. At this moment I'm thinking of my eighth- or ninth-grade English teacher, who introduced me to Samuel Johnson. She made the *Rambler* and the *Idler,* where so many of Johnson's essays were published, part of my vocabulary of knowledge. Her anecdotes about some of Johnson's peculiar physical habits awakened a fascination with the man himself.

Later I came to know something about Samuel Johnson, the lexicographer. His *Dictionary of the English Language* is still a model of both scholarship and independent thinking. I also learned of Samuel Johnson the novelist and poet; of Samuel Johnson, who set the standard for biography in his studies of the poets; and of Samuel Johnson whose own biography (by James Boswell) is so well known. Then, of course, there is Samuel Johnson, the raconteur, the person you would most enjoy as a guest–though an unpredictable one–at your dinner party.

But the Samuel Johnson who interests me most is Samuel Johnson the Christian, the man who considered his faith the most important single feature in his wide-ranging life. Johnson whets my interest all the more because he possessed and practiced his faith at a time when religion was not popular among people of Johnson's class and style.

## Samuel Johnson's Background

Let me tell you a little about the man. He was born in Lichfield, England, on September 7, 1709. Sickly from his birth, Johnson developed a tubercular infection of the skin early in his infancy. The infection eventually marred his face to a degree that made him shocking to those meeting him for the first time. He attended Oxford University for two years, but had to leave when he ran out of money.

He then entered on a period of hand-to-mouth existence, as he depended upon publishing occasional pieces in periodicals for his income. Nevertheless, his writing soon began to develop a following. The publication of his Dictionary in 1755 brought him recognition as the leading literary figure of his time. Even today we often refer to that period as "the Age of Johnson." A type of writing that seems to resemble his is defined in literary studies as "Johnsonese." Very few people have ever made such an impression on language and literature as the man Samuel Johnson.

## Samuel Johnson in Person

Although somewhat physically prepossessing because of his size, Johnson could also at first meeting, be repugnant because of his facial appearance and his sometimes grotesque mannerisms. He had "almost perpetual convulsive movements" of hands, lips, feet or knees, and sometimes all at the same time. He picked at his fingers almost constantly. He had lost part of his vision in a disease in infancy, and by adult life was very myopic, with sight in only one eye. Yet his eyes were "so wild, so piercing, and at Time so fierce" that fear was the emotion often struck in those who watched him.[2]

Nevertheless, his conversation and his insights captivated people. He had ideas and expressed them with extraordinary eloquence. When he was twenty-six, he married Elizabeth Porter, who was twenty years older. None of Johnson's friends could see what he saw in her, but he considered it "a love marriage." A number of his most beautiful prayers were written on various anniversaries of his wife's death. Although he never re-married, he was a great favorite with women, who sought out his company at all social occasions.

## Samuel Johnson's Convictions

No one was ever in doubt as to Johnson's convictions. A person of strong opinions, especially as regarded moral conduct, he never tailored his opinions to win the favor of persons whose power might have benefited him. In the last paragraph of his last essay in the *Rambler* he reflected on what he had tried to do with his essays. He said that he had intended them to "be found exactly conformable to the precepts of Christianity and without any accommodation to the licentiousness and levity of the present age."[3] Mind you, the *Rambler* was not a religious periodical but a general publication aimed at a thoughtful audience.

While he loved nothing better than to eat and talk with friends, he never sacrificed conviction for the sake of friendship. The general mood among the intellectuals of Johnson's day was one of "open scoffing" at religion, but as philosopher Elton Trueblood has said, Johnson dared to go "against the main currents of his days."

## Samuel Johnson's Conversion

Johnson's deep religious convictions began in 1729, when he was twenty years old. They remained his convictions to his death at age seventy-five. One factor in Johnson's spiritual awakening was his reading of William Law's *Serious Call to a Devout and Holy Life,* a book that also influenced John Wesley, the founder of Methodism. A student at Oxford when he began reading Law's book, Johnson expected to find it dull or to be amused by it. Instead, "I found Law quite an overmatch for me," and with that he began an earnest, rational investigation of Christianity. James Boswell wrote much later, "From this time forward, religion was the predominant object of his [Johnson's] thoughts."[4]

Every Christian pilgrimage is singular. Converts may stop at certain similar points and may certainly come to strategic conclusions, but the path between those points and the route to the conclusions are probably as individual as our fingerprints. God begins with us where we are and works with the stuff we bring to the journey. Johnson's unfolding journey is notable for the fact that he never turned back and never denied any of his basic convictions. But he knew the meaning of struggle.

## Samuel Johnson's Christian Struggle

In fact, struggle might be the word most descriptive of Johnson's personality. His nature was to question everything. One might almost say he was the quintessential scholar, in that he was never satisfied that the answers gotten or the conclusions reached could be considered final. Because of this temperament, he often questioned his own salvation. Nearing death, he wondered whether he had fulfilled the conditions on which salvation is granted. When, on an earlier occasion, someone asked if he were forgetting the merits of our Redeemer Christ, Johnson answered, "I do not forget the merits of my Redeemer; but my Redeemer has said that he will set some on his right hand and some on his left."[5]

While he questioned his own salvation, he questioned nothing about the scriptures or the teachings of the Anglican Church. William Hogarth, whose paintings have helped millions to visualize the eighteenth century, once said that Johnson was not content with believing the Bible, he seemed resolved "to believe nothing *but* the Bible."[6] He was in every sense an orthodox Christian.

Believing as he did in the justice of God, he therefore believed in immortality. He believed in the objective power of prayer and maintained a faithful prayer life. He saw the Bible as the Word of God, divinely inspired; and he believed in free will, the power of the individual to determine his or her own fate.

## Samuel Johnson's Beliefs about Sin

Johnson wouldn't be popular among the literary circle of our time, particularly in his strong beliefs about sin. He believed that we humans are strongly inclined to sin and that because of this, even our most earnest efforts are likely to be tainted with evil. Even the finest of us need continual reminders of our duty, and the best of us need the help of the church if we are to live honorably. We humans are universally corrupt, Johnson said; the only difference is that we are corrupt in different degrees.

As for his own soul's struggle, Johnson labored especially with an inclination to sloth. He was a person who loved the company of others and was inclined therefore to stay up late eating and talking. Then he would sleep late in the morning. This caused him much self-condemnation. So in his prayers he would ask forgiveness because "I have this day neglected the duty which Thou hast assigned to it, and suffered the hours, of which I must give account, to pass away without any endeavour to accomplish thy will, or to promote my own salvation."[7] And again, "Grant, O Lord, that I may not lavish away the life which Thou hast given me on useless trifles"; instead, he prayed that he might "obtain, in all my undertakings, such success as will most promote thy glory, and the salvation of my own soul."[8]

This hunger for a better use of his time was especially mentioned in Johnson's prayers on his birthdays and on New Year's, the times when he reflected on his life and wished he were doing better with it. So on his twenty-ninth birthday he prayed "to redeem the time which I have spent in Sloth, Vanity, and Wickedness." Twenty years later he prayed to "improve the time which is yet before me," even as he repented of "the days misspent in idleness and folly." At the New Year of 1780, now a man in his seventy-first year, he prayed, "let me be no longer idle, no longer sinful; but give me rectitude of thought and constancy of action." This was a man who struggled for holiness and saw the issue of holiness especially in his use of time. From all evidence, he fought this battle to the very end.

### Samuel Johnson and Personal Relationships

If Samuel Johnson often lost the battle with sloth, he conducted himself well in his treatment of others. Often an impatient man, he didn't suffer fools gladly, but he had a heart for human infirmity. In an age where social structures were praised and those without standing were easily despised, Johnson insisted that "a decent provision for the poor is the true test of civilization."[9] Only an Old Testament prophet could have said it better. When an acquaintance said giving halfpennies to common beggars was a waste because they only put it into gin and tobacco, Johnson replied with broad sympathy, "And why should they be denied such sweeteners of their existence?"[10] Mrs. Thrale, who knew Johnson as well as anyone (with the possible exception of Boswell), said, "Mr. Johnson has more Tenderness for Poverty than any other Man I ever know." She listed the poor who took lodging with him, adding that "he also kept a sort of odd Levee for distress's Authors, breaking Booksellers, and in short every body that has even the lowest Pretensions to Literature in Distress."[11]

He was particularly sensitive to his servants. One was a freed slave, Francis Barber. Mrs. Thrale noted that although Johnson thought of Negroes as "a race naturally inferior" (a prevalent conception of the times), he always sided with Francis in household disputes, because he suspected that others took advantage of him.

After Johnson's wife, Tetty, died, he brought into his home her blind friend, Anna Williams and cared for her. She poured tea for his guests. Since she couldn't see when the cups were filled, she measured the fullness by her finger. Catherine Chambers was a servant to Johnson's mother for forty-three years. As she lay dying, Catherine asked Johnson for prayer. He knelt by her bed to ask God's care of her soul. Trueblood, wrote, "Here is one of the truly noble scenes of our history—the leading man of letters of his nation and century kneeling in humble faith by the bedside of his mother's servant."[12]

I am always especially impressed by Johnson's kindness to another writer of his century, Christopher Smart. Smart was a person of extraordinary talent, which for a time he dissipated. After a time of illness and mental depression, he was led to faith in Christ. He then became so earnest that he was likely to stop anywhere to pray on his knees, on the street and in public places. His former literary associates quickly dropped him, except for Johnson, who observed that "it is greater madness not to pray at all than to pray as Smart did," yet no one calls their madness of neglect into question. Eventually Christopher Smart was confined in a series of asylums. Samuel Johnson was the only literary friend to visit him. For a period of time, Johnson wrote numerous articles over Smart's name to fulfill contractual commitments and to provide income for Smart's wife and children. Johnson said, "I'd as lief pray with Kit Smart as with anyone else."[13]

## Samuel Johnson's Way with Words

Samuel Johnson was a person who knew words about as well as anyone in any generation. As one of his contemporaries said, Johnson could say "even the most common things in the *newest* manner."[14] As someone who loves words, I honor Johnson for this. I envy those who enjoyed his company. I'm no longer disposed to sit up late talking, but I'd change my ways if there were opportunity to visit with Sam Johnson!

But I admire him most for the earnest piety with which he employed words in prayer and for the consistency of his Christian faith that caused him to live as he believed and spoke. He was a genius with words, but more than that, he was a man of his word. Please God, may his tribe increase.

# CHAPTER 9

# John Newton

*Amazing!*

If any one piece of music cuts across levels of taste and culture, age and life style, it is, of all things, a hymn, "Amazing Grace." It confounds us. About a generation ago, when a major North American denomination decided to eliminate this song from its new hymnal, it suddenly became part of popular music's hit parade. We have come to associate it with the rather mournful sound of the bagpipes, but we're just as likely to hear it in the style of bluegrass, country western, jazz, or even a bit of rock, as well as of course, standard piano or organ renditions in churches of almost every size and denomination. I venture that those churches that don't have "Amazing Grace" in their hymnal manage to produce copies for their congregation or simply trust that people can recall a verse or two from memory.

## Introducing John Newton

But what of the person who wrote the song? Sometimes the people who write a poem, a novel, or a song are not themselves particularly interesting. Not so with John Newton, who gave us the words for "Amazing Grace." He's the kind of person qualified to write, "that saved a wretch like me," though his definition of a wretch might not conform to yours or mine.

### Basic Background

John Newton was born July 24, 1725, in Wapping, London, on the north bank of the River Thames. His mother, a devout woman

who taught John to read when he was four and introduced him to
Latin at age five, died when he was only seven. Soon thereafter, his
father placed him in a boarding school, where he encountered
schooling very different from that offered by his mother. At age eleven,
he joined his father, a sea captain, on a trip that lasted over two years.
Life became something of a downward spiral from that point. At
times he returned to the faith his mother had so earnestly urged upon
him, but a seaman's life was a poor nursery for a young soul. He
spent several years in the slave trade and was himself "a slave to
slaves" at one time.

On February 1, 1750, John married Mary Catlett, who blessed
his life in numerous ways for the next forty years. As his faith grew,
John entered holy orders in the Anglican Church, becoming a deacon
on April 29, 1764. Although he wrote many hymns and published a
variety of sermons and treatises, his place in popular memory rests
with a hymn he wrote in late December, 1772, now known around
the world as "Amazing Grace." John Newton died December 21, 1807.

### Communities of Interest

When a song is sung in virtually every part of the world and is
arranged for everything from symphonic performances to folk,
bluegrass, rock, and black gospel, the author of it clearly holds interest
for almost everyone. Obviously, you will want the congregation to
sing this hymn at some point in the service. If possible, have it sung
or played in one or more styles different from those the group
ordinarily experiences. Since all of Newton's verses rarely appear in
our hymnals, there is value in including the original work in its entirety.
You may wish to isolate the last verse ("When we've been there ten
thousand years"), which was added long after Newton's death.

**SERMON** _____

# John Newton: *Amazing!*

## Scripture Lesson: 1 Corinthians 15:3–10

In December, 1999, when the whole world was fascinated by a once-
in-a-millennium change in the calendar, *USA Today* offered a list of
one hundred things that should be saved in a time capsule as the
essence of the twentieth century. The list included two songs—"Auld
Lang Syne" and "Amazing Grace." Three years earlier, the Music

Educators' National Conference drew up a list of forty-two songs it deemed essential to be learned by coming generations. "Amazing Grace" was there. Thirty-three songs stood among five thousand names, phrases, dates, and concepts that E. D. Hirsch offered in his 1987 book, *Cultural Literacy,* as essential for every American to know. Only five of the songs were religious—two Christmas carols, two spirituals, and one hymn. The hymn was "Amazing Grace."

When I give you these facts, you're likely to answer, "That's interesting; in fact, very interesting. But I'm not surprised." The data reflect what you yourself might have voted if you had drawn up any such list.

## John Newton's Background

On further thought, you begin to wonder. Simple as it seems to be, this hymn is packed full of theology. It offers glimpses of grace, sin, salvation, prevenient grace, the nature of the Christian life, death, eternity, and the character of God. Yet ironically, it has been included in the repertoire of musicians who don't even think of it as a religious song, including some who would identify themselves as agnostic. Who in the world gave us such a song as this?

His name was John Newton, and his story is as amazing as his song. He was born July 24, 1725, in London on the north bank of the River Thames, not far from the Tower of London. His father was a sea captain, and his mother was a devout Christian who prayed her son would someday grow up to be a minister. Her prayer was answered abundantly, though she didn't live to see it. Nevertheless, she set the direction by teaching her son to read when he was four and by beginning his study of Latin when he was five. Sadly, she died from tuberculosis when John was only seven.

The boy then entered a difficult period, perhaps the most difficult in a life that knew many difficulties. His father remarried shortly after the mother's death and placed John in a boarding school. It was the kind of institution memorialized in Charles Dickens's novels. John was so thoroughly broken by the system that he began to lose the power of his remarkable young memory and began to see himself as stupid. When he was eleven, he went to sea with his father, on a voyage that lasted more than two years. I suspect that's one way for a boy to grow up rapidly, but not an easy one.

## John Newton's Spiritual Struggles

One of the memorable lines in "Amazing Grace" says, "'Twas grace that taught my heart to fear, / And grace my fears relieved."

Some of the fears that quickened John's sensitivity to God came during his years on board ship. Several times his life was miraculously spared. After each such experience, John became more attentive to his conduct, but in each instance, he allowed himself to slip back into a way of life that was indifferent to God and to moral restraint. His shipboard reading, in which he could invest endless hours, sometimes drew him toward God and sometimes just the opposite. Later John would feel that through it all God was at work in his life.

John's father retired from sea duty in 1742. John didn't desire a life at sea, but it was the one work for which he was trained. He made things worse through missteps and arrogance. Eventually, he got transferred to a ship bound for Sierra Leone, where it would pick up slaves. Later in life, Newton said that in this period he became "exceedingly vile," though he offered no particulars. On such ships, slave girls were often taken for sexual pleasure. Newton doesn't specifically say that he did so, but leaves broad hints. He described himself later as a person who was "a slave to every customary vice."[1]

Newton then chose to work for a slave trader, intending to develop his skills in that ugly business. But through a series of misadventures and a time of illness, he became at odds with the slave trader's mistress, an African woman of royal family. She worked systematically to humiliate Newton, sometimes feeding him scraps from her dish and taunting him in his physical helplessness. When Newton wrote his own epitaph, many years later, he described himself as having once been "a servant of slaves in Africa," referring to this period.

Newton blamed no one but himself for his troubles. He recognized that a long series of his own irresponsible deeds had gotten him in trouble and had alienated him from so many. During this period Newton became afflicted with what was probably rheumatoid arthritis. It troubled him the rest of his life. He saw it as "a needful memento of the services and wages of sin."[2]

Then Newton got a better position. He was soon comfortable, so comfortable he wasn't sure he wanted to leave. When another opportunity came, only one factor persuaded him, the prospect of bringing an English girl, Mary Catlett, into his life. At this time God was only intermittently in his thoughts, and blasphemy marked his life more than did prayer. The scriptures say the work of the Holy Spirit is like the wind: it "blows where it chooses, and you hear the sound of it, but you do not know where it comes from or where it goes" (Jn. 3:8). John Newton's life fulfills that scripture as well as anybody's—and on the other hand, probably better than no one's.

His experiences were more dramatic than most of us know, but in total and in outcome, they were much like those of any person who finally confesses Christ as Lord.

## John Newton's Conversion

As Newton drew nearer a lasting decision, miraculous escapes from peril were interwoven with continuing confusion about his beliefs. On the positive side, he was especially moved by the devotional classic *The Imitation of Christ,* by Thomas á Kempis. See the parts coming together: love for a woman, persuading him to be a better human being; perils on land and sea that make him think his life is being spared for a purpose; and a book that drives him to honest thought. Then, add in all those elements that can never be measured, such as the influence of his mother in the first seven years of his life, and her prayers offered on his behalf. Consider, too, all the negative, corrupting experiences and pursuits that gave Newton a point of contrast with the Christian life. Put all these factors together, and call it amazing. Amazing Grace.

## John Newton's Courtship

When John Newton finally got back to England, he had not seen Mary Catlett for three years. He realized he was not the kind of son-in-law a respectable family would seek. Even if the Catletts knew nothing of his unstable ways, he was penniless. The company that owned his ship had declared bankruptcy, and he had nothing for his years of work. When her parents finally permitted Newton to see Mary, he was so at a loss for words that he could ask only if he might write her a letter. He produced an eloquent appeal for "a little of your charity, one morsel for God's sake before I am quite starved."[3] When he received Mary's reply, he feared to open the letter. When he did, he found that though she wrote "in the most cautious terms," she was not rejecting him.

Newton returned to the sea on a slave ship. From our vantage point this seems an unlikely place for a person to seriously begin a Christian life, but it was more complicated for Newton. Many of our convictions are tempered by the times in which we live, more, no doubt, than we know. In Newton's day, only the Quakers and Anabaptists openly opposed slavery. Some Christians believed that by enslaving Africans they were giving them a chance to hear the gospel. In such a confusing theological context Newton went about his work in a ship that eventually brought its cargo to Charleston, South Carolina.

When he returned to England, Newton was at last ready to make a face-to-face request for Mary's hand. She refused his request twice: then with more persuading, she accepted. On February 1, 1750, they were married at St. Margaret's Church in Rochester, Kent. The girl he had first met when he was seven and she was three was now his wife.

## John Newton the Sea Captain

Three months later, he returned to the sea, this time as captain of a slave ship. He began each day with at least an hour of prayer in his cabin. He brought his entire crew to a church service each Sunday, with hymns and Anglican liturgy. In a letter to his childhood minister, he confided his interest in writing a book of "advices and devotions" for seamen because he had seen that they weren't well served by conventional books of prayer.

Nevertheless, he was in the slave business. Biographers sometimes marvel at the incongruity between the daily devotions Newton pursued, the sensitive letters he wrote to his wife, and the condition of the slaves in the hold just below him. He felt it his duty to provide circumstances as humane as possible for the slaves. Not until years later did he fully recognize the evil of slavery.

## John Newton's Call

An unexpected attack of illness (Newton called it "apoplexy") forced him to give up the sea. He was given a job in August, 1755, as tide surveyor in Liverpool. There the evangelical fervor that was spreading through England came to influence him. As people learned of his remarkable experiences, they frequently invited him to preach. This led to a sense of call. He wanted to serve the Church of England, but unfortunately, he lacked the education required. Although at first he was rejected, Lord Dartmouth, an influential leader in both the religious and political community, saw to his appointment as curate-in-charge at Olney, a quiet community of some 2,500 persons. On April 29, 1764, Newton became a deacon in the Anglican Church and two months later moved to Olney.

## John Newton the Deacon and Hymn Writer

In 1767, William Cowper moved to Olney. This is a notable date in Christian hymnody. Cowper had been converted some two years earlier. He and Newton became the closest of friends. Out of the friendship of Cowper and Newton came the famous *Olney Hymns,* a collection that includes several hymns still sung around the world today.

Cowper was a brilliant young man who eventually played a key role in the Romantic Movement in English poetry, but he was also plagued by periods of extreme depression, when he was unable to be employed. Newton had written some poetry earlier, but only under Cowper's influence did poetry become a major form of expression and ministry. At the same time, Newton's friendship and extraordinary pastoral care kept Cowper sane and, at least part of the time, very productive.

## John Newton and "Amazing Grace"

Newton's most famous hymn, "Amazing Grace," was most likely written in the last days of 1772 for use with his New Year's sermon for 1773. Newton's practice, once his poetic abilities were set loose, was to write a new hymn each week to be used with the sermon of the week. In the last week of 1772, Newton was doing what many of us are inclined to do at a year's end: he was reviewing the course of his life. He marveled especially at the past seventeen years and the grace that had brought him to his present state of effective, fruitful living.

The hymn was probably sung that day without accompaniment, to one of the tunes familiar to the Olney congregation. The melody that now seems inseparable from the words wasn't associated with "Amazing Grace" until 1835. A verse that is now a favorite with many– "When we've been there ten thousand years, / Bright shining as the sun"–wasn't part of the original and wasn't written by Newton. We don't know the author of these lines. They first appeared in print in Harriet Beecher Stowe's antislavery novel, *Uncle Tom's Cabin* in 1852. It is popularly assumed that the words were added to the hymn as sung by slaves, in their worship. If so, it is a providential conclusion to a hymn written by a former slave trader.

## John Newton's Emerging Views on Slavery

Some key changes in our lives come like a bolt of lightning, but more evolve over a period of time. The latter is the case with Newton's attitude toward slavery. Things were happening. In 1773, the Countess of Huntingdon (who had been influential in Lord Dartmouth's conversion) financed the printing of a book of poems by former slave Phyllis Wheatley, the first book published by an African American. The Countess dedicated it to Lord Dartmouth.

The following year John Wesley published his vigorous "Thoughts on Slavery." In 1781, Newton's close friend, William Cowper, began writing poems attacking slavery. Then, somewhere in the mid-1780s, Newton publicly committed himself to the abolition movement.

His influence was made more powerful by his relationship with William Wilberforce, the genius of the antislavery movement in England. A brilliant member of Parliament, Wilberforce was at first cautious in seeking out John Newton. By this time Newton had moved from Olney to St. Mary Woolnoth, in London, where his influence was greatly multiplied. However, he was also highly controversial because of his evangelical views. When Wilberforce sought Newton's counsel, Newton urged him to stay in politics and use his influence for God. It was sound counsel. Wilberforce probably had as beneficent an influence on England's moral conscience as any single statesman in its history. Newton was a sustaining element in Wilberforce's life for many years.

In time, Newton became an influence on many lives. His range was phenomenal. Both the simple village folk and the movers and shakers of his time sought him out. His letters of encouragement and counsel are gems of pastoral wisdom, as his letters to Mary are the essence of a passionately devoted spouse. A largely self-educated man, he became recognized as a true scholar. His London pulpit became a favorite place for both the earnest seeker and the simply curious.

## John Newton's Legacy

But Newton never forgot who he was. The apostle Paul described himself as "unfit to be called an apostle" because he had persecuted the church, but confident that God's grace toward him had "not been in vain" (1 Cor. 15:9–10). Newton chose something of the same theme in the epitaph he prepared for himself: "John Newton, Clerk, once an Infidel and Libertine…by the rich mercy of our Lord and Saviour Jesus Christ, preserved, restored, pardoned, and appointed to preach the faith he had long laboured to destroy…"

John Newton lived out an amazing life. But like Paul, he knew that his story was simply amazing grace.

# CHAPTER 10

# A Novel, a Novelist, and a Prophet

## *Jonah, Meet Moby Dick!*

Some people say *Moby Dick* is the greatest novel ever written. Limiting the field of judgment, others say that if there is, in truth, a great American novel, this is it. Nevertheless, the name of the author, Herman Melville, is probably not known to a majority in any congregation. So it's hazardous to announce that Herman Melville is going to be the subject of a sermon or even that you're going to talk about a novel. I've chosen, therefore, to be a little playful in titling this sermon, as you will see momentarily.

Early in my university education, I came upon a twentieth-century philosopher who said that some of the best philosophy was being written not by professional philosophers but by novelists. Not only do I concur with that judgment, I would also like to add to it. I believe some of the best *theology* has been, and continues to be, written by novelists. I'm thinking of C. S. Lewis, Charles Williams, J. R. R. Tolkien, and Flannery O'Connor, not just of novelists such as Dorothy Sayers and G. K. Chesterton, who chose to write some specific theological works. Indeed, one thinks of the great Russian novelists, who seemed haunted by issues of God and sin, and the continuing number who use the scriptures as a point of focus or of departure. One might say that any novelist who deals seriously with what John Steinbeck called "the only story," the issue of good and evil, is in at least a measure, a theologian. By any measure, Melville qualifies.

## Introducing Herman Melville

### Basic Background

Herman Melville was born August l, 1819, in New York City. In 1839 he shipped out as a cabin boy on a merchant ship for Liverpool. In that and subsequent voyages, he accumulated the materials that fed several of his novels, including his masterpiece, *Moby Dick,* published in 1851. He dedicated it to Nathaniel Hawthorne, with whom for a time he had a close friendship. He died in 1891. Only since his death has his stature as a novelist become recognized.

### Communities of Interest

This sermon obviously appeals to those persons who love literature and also to those who are particularly sensitive to some of the issues with which many thoughtful persons struggle. Melville is a kind of icon to some persons who find kinship with his inner turmoil. A pastor who has gained a hearing for thoughtful insight might well do a short series, perhaps four Sundays, on specific novelists, past and present. I dared such a venture through a Lenten season many years ago. I enjoyed the benefit of a university community (Madison, Wisconsin), but my congregation ran the gamut of ages and occupations and education, so it was important to present these sermons in a form and with an appeal that was clearly not limited to an imagined intellectual elite.

**SERMON** _____

# Herman Melville: *Jonah, Meet Moby Dick!*

## Scripture Lesson: Jonah 1:1–17

Let me venture an opinion. I can't prove it, but I'm certain it would be even more difficult for someone to disprove it. I contend that the two best known fish in the world are Moby Dick and the fish that did business with the Old Testament prophet Jonah. There's irony in this bit of speculation because, of course, Moby Dick is a fictional character, while the fish in the Jonah story is not really the point of the story, even if people insist on making it so. Further, a good number of biblical scholars feel that Jonah's fish was himself a character in a holy parable rather than an actual creature. I won't get into that issue in any depth. I only submit that these two notable fish have several things in common. And I will insist that even in this age of amusement parks that specialize in sea creatures and of heralded oceanic exploration, no fish can compare with Moby Dick and Jonah's great fish for a massive audience.

## Introducing Jonah

Let me tell you about Jonah. Almost surely, you know the story so I won't go into many details. Once there was a prophet of God named Jonah. He was probably a rather good man, and he was clearly a gifted preacher. Like many of us, he tended to be narrow in his sympathies. When God directed him to preach to the people of Nineveh, he objected. The people of Nineveh were not nice people; especially, they weren't nice if you were an Israelite. So Jonah threw out his divine traveling orders and booked passage in the opposite direction.

While he was asleep in his cabin, a great storm arose. The superstitious mariners cast lots to find out why they were in such unexpected trouble, and the lot fell on Jonah. He quite bravely told the sailors that if they would cast him overboard, the storm would cease. They did so, even if reluctantly, and sure enough, the storm ended. "But the LORD provided a large fish to swallow up Jonah" (Jon. 1:17). Jonah spent three days and nights in the belly of the fish. There he came to his senses. I suspect a setting of that sort would convince almost anyone to think and to pray. The fish "spewed Jonah out upon the dry land" (Jon. 2:10). Jonah proceeded to do the job to which God had called him originally, and the people of Nineveh responded to his preaching with sincere repentance. But as the story ends, Jonah wasn't a happy man. Even with this remarkable experience, he still didn't really like the people of Nineveh. What's more, he obviously couldn't understand how God could have mercy on them.

## Introducing *Moby Dick*

The Bible tells this story, including Jonah's prayer, in less than two pages. Herman Melville took a great many more pages for *Moby Dick*–in fact, more than six hundred pages in the edition that I read most recently. And yet, in a sense, the story can be told in a paragraph.

*Moby Dick* is the story of a veteran sea captain, Ahab, who has spent forty of his fifty-eight years in whaling ships. In fact, late in the story, he says that since first putting to sea he has probably spent all but three years of his life on the waters of our planet. Some years before, a white whale, whom we know as Moby Dick, tore off one of

Ahab's legs. Ever since, Ahab has been driven by a single goal–to get Moby Dick.

The author is quite leisurely in bringing us to the climax of the story. It isn't until perhaps the last twenty-five pages that the showdown finally comes. Until then, Herman Melville gives us an astonishing amount of information about whales, the sea, and the whaling industry. In fact, he gives us more than most of us care to know. Recently I discussed this novel with two well-educated and rather perceptive persons. They both confessed that they had started the novel several times but had never finished it. They just weren't that interested in fish. Not even in Moby Dick.

If you don't get impatient with the facts and speculation concerning whales, you find that the story rivets your attention. Captain Ahab is such a powerful man, yet so weak in the face of his obsession. He can stare down the toughest of his officers and the most uncivilized of his crew, but he can't shake himself free of a whale that he intends to bring to its fate. He will travel thousands of miles over the oceans of the world in its pursuit. The captain of another ship begs Ahab to assist him in finding his son, whose boat has been lost. Ahab coldly refuses, ordering the man off his ship. For Ahab only one thing matters–to get the white whale.

Max Otto, a professor of philosophy in the first half of the twentieth century, often told his students that some of the best philosophy was being written, not by professional philosophers, but by novelists. There's little doubt but that this novel, *Moby Dick,* is full of philosophy and that its author intended it to be so. It has even more to say about theology–that is, about God. Philosophy can try to skirt around the issue of God, but, of course, the main business of theology is God and all that relates to God.

## Herman Melville's Background

Perhaps at this point we should talk for a while about the man who wrote the novel, Herman Melville. Melville lived at a time when literature was coming into its own in America. America had earlier had some outstanding writers, but they were more likely to be preachers, theologians, and political philosophers. Americans who wanted fine creative writing in their own tongue looked to England. Then came a marvelous period with such names as Henry Wadsworth Longfellow, Oliver Wendell Holmes, James Russell Lowell, Ralph Waldo Emerson, Henry David Thoreau, Nathaniel Hawthorne, and Herman Melville–all those people your high school English teachers required you to read! Some people who ought to know identify Melville as the most powerful of the whole lot.

Melville was born in New York City in 1819. He moved with his family to Albany, New York, when he was eleven. Two years later his father died, leaving the family deeply in debt. During the next few years Herman worked on a farm, went to sea, taught school, and tried to write. Then, at twenty-one, he boarded a whaling boat for the South Seas. This became his education, his Yale and his Harvard, as he put it.

## Herman Melville's Theology

Though Melville's formal education was limited, he read widely in philosophy, religion, and literature. For a period of time he was perhaps Nathaniel Hawthorne's closest friend. They talked "about time and eternity, things of this world and of the next, and books and publishers, and all possible and impossible matters."[1] I would like to have sat in on some of those visits between Hawthorne and Melville, two intelligent, disturbed, and creative souls! Melville dedicated the novel considered his masterpiece to Hawthorne.

Melville never went to theological seminary, but he knew his Bible as well as did a great many preachers. The opening sentence of *Moby Dick,* "Call me Ishmael," is clearly meant to have symbolic significance. Ishmael was the son born to Abraham and his wife's slave girl Hagar (Gen. 16:11–15). Thus Ishmael is always an outsider, a man who doesn't belong to the chosen line or to the divine promise. Melville ends the novel with a one-page epilogue that begins with a line from the Old Testament book of Job: "I alone have escaped to tell you" (Job 1:15, 17,19). In between the reader encounters frequent quotations from scripture as well as passing allusions that only a fairly good Bible student would catch. Of course, the lead character has a biblical name, Ahab. That isn't the sort of name a pious parent would give to a child, because Ahab was one of Israel's most notorious kings, husband to the wicked Jezebel, and weak and wicked in his own right. When a biblically knowledgeable author names his hero Ahab, we know he's trying to tell us something.

## The *Moby Dick* Struggle

The book was a struggle all the way. In June of 1850, Melville wrote his English publisher that he could expect the book by late autumn. By the end of June, 1851, Melville wrote to Nathaniel Hawthorne that he was now preparing to "end the book." He complained that it was "hell-fire in which the whole book is broiled." When at last the book was finished, Melville was sure he had "written a wicked book."[2]

I wouldn't call it a wicked book, unless one judges a book to be wicked because the author hasn't found his destination or hasn't been able to reach a conclusion that satisfies him. It's interesting that, of all the books in the Bible, Melville was most fascinated by Job and Ecclesiastes. Without a doubt, Melville was on a search. His mind was such that he couldn't be satisfied with easy answers. If he had met the kind of Christian (and he probably did) who told him, "You just have to trust God," or, "Whatever happens, it must be the will of God," Melville would have walked away in frustration. As he said after a lecture by Emerson, Melville loved "men who *dive*. Any fish can swim near the surface, but it takes a great whale to go downstairs five miles or more."[3] I think some people by nature are more easily satisfied than are others. Just as surely, some of those who struggle for answers, sometimes never find real peace of mind.

In the story of Jonah, the great fish is only a supporting character. He is a factor in bringing the plot to pass, but he isn't a leader in the plot. The lead characters in Jonah's story are God and Jonah. But in *Moby Dick*, the whale is the lead character. For the "superstitiously inclined," he was "ubiquitous." That's a minor version of the nature of God, who is omnipresent. Other sailors had come to think that Moby Dick was immortal because it seemed no one could capture or kill him.

To Ahab, who was irreversibly on his trail, Moby Dick was "all evil…visibly personified."[4] All of those closest to Captain Ahab plead with him to give up his pursuit of the great white whale, but with "fatal pride" Ahab goes on until he destroys himself, his ship, and the crew entrusted to his leadership. In other words, if Moby Dick was "all evil," Captain Ahab at last became as evil as the thing he was resolved to destroy. I wonder how often, in lesser matters, people have become as evil as the enemy they despised. Perhaps this is the ultimate terror of evil, that those who fight it sometimes are captured by it even as they think they are defeating it. This is the story of those who manipulate to cope with manipulators, those who become hateful as they fight hatred, and those who seek to root out impurity by impure means.

I should note that only one character in *Moby Dick* portrays Christianity in truly admirable light. He is Father Mapple, pastor of Whaleman's Chapel in New Bedford. In introducing Father Mapple, Melville describes preaching the way I and all of my clergy colleagues wish to fulfill it. He says that the pulpit is "a self-containing stronghold" with "a perennial well of water." Because "the pulpit is ever this earth's foremost part, all the rest comes in its rear; the pulpit leads the world.…Yes, the world's a ship on its passage out, and not a voyage complete; and the pulpit is its prow."[5]

## A Question at the End

The book of Jonah and *Moby Dick* have something very special in common besides giving us the world's two most famous fish. Both books end with a question. Not a spoken question, but an implied and unavoidable one. God was asking Jonah to realize that God's divine grace was large enough to include even the people of Nineveh, but as the story ends, we don't know how Jonah responded. That's the point of the book. In its original writing, it was to remind the Jewish people that God's purpose in calling them was to reach all the world, including their enemies. The same message comes to us as Christians.

As I read *Moby Dick*, I wonder if Herman Melville's great questions were ever answered to his satisfaction. Did he conclude that God is good and gracious even though evil is often so monstrous? I find myself pondering these words in the latter portion of the novel. "The truest of all men was the Man of Sorrows, and the truest of all books is Solomon's, and Ecclesiastes is fine hammered steel of woe. 'All is vanity.' ALL." Then Melville goes on to say, "And there is a Catskill eagle in some souls that can alike dive down into the blackest gorges, and soar out of them again and become invisible in the sunny spaces."[6]

Was Melville saying that he hoped he was one of those who, having dived down into the blackest gorges, would someday also soar out to sunny spaces? He saw "All is vanity" as the truest word he knew. But he also saw Jesus Christ as "the truest of all men." I wonder if, in the end, his weight fell more on Christ than on vanity? I need not tell you where I want your weight and mine to fall.

# CHAPTER 11

# Frederick Douglass
## *Living Up to Our Name*

Most of us will admit readily, even if with pain, that the church doesn't always live up to its own teachings. We bear the name of Christ, but we don't always bring honor to that name. This realization gets new force in the story of Frederick Douglass. It isn't by any means the only lesson in his story, but it is an important one.

### Introducing Frederick Douglass

Douglass is one of the truly towering figures of the mid-nineteenth century. If we project what history tells us of his charisma and his platform genius, we can speculate rather wildly as to the political heights he might have reached in the twenty-first century. But caught as we are in a constant rush of news and almost-news, we can easily forget that a person like Frederick Douglass ever lived.

So his story ought to be told whether on Martin Luther King Day, Independence Day Sunday, or simply to make some continuing points about the wonders of genius and how it comes to exist. His story shows the power of human personality and the force of indomitable convictions. Along the way, the importance of the church living up to its name comes into play.

### *Basic Background*

Frederick Douglass (Frederick Augustus Washington Bailey) was born in February, 1817 or 1818, in Tuckahoe, Maryland, the son of a slave mother and a white father he never knew. He worked as a house servant, a field hand, and then in a shipyard. With the help of his owner's wife and with his own remarkable persistence, he learned to read and write. In 1838 he fled to New York City and from there to New Bedford, Massachusetts. For three years he worked in a variety of menial jobs, along the way dropping his two middle names and changing his last name to Douglass to foil slave hunters.

In 1841, he was asked to speak extemporaneously at an antislavery convention. His natural eloquence thrust him into a new career with the Massachusetts Anti-Slavery Society. During a two-year speaking tour of Great Britain and Ireland, he raised the money to buy his freedom and to start a newspaper, which he published in Rochester, New York, from 1847 to 1860. His stature and insight brought him to Washington often during the Civil War for consultation with President Lincoln. From 1881 to 1886 he was Recorder of Deeds in the District of Columbia, and from 1889 to 1891, U.S. minister and consul general to Haiti.

### Communities of Interest

Frederick Douglass appeals to people with differing interests:

1. students of history for his role in the antislavery movement and in the Civil War
2. lovers of literature, especially biography, for his remarkable autobiography
3. people fascinated by human personality and by the question of what makes us what we are
4. the African American community for his role in giving them freedom and identity
5. anyone with a passion for justice and equality

**SERMON** _____

# Frederick Douglass: *Living Up to Our Name*

## Scripture Lesson: Matthew 23:1–3, 23–28

I love the church. I began attending its services when I was still in my mother's womb. I was brought as an infant to its altar for baptism. I was so nurtured by the Sunday school that two generations later I can still name a dozen people who led me through Sunday school quarterlies and memory verses. My first real heroes were the evangelists who visited our town. I have spent all the years of my adult life preaching in churches–churches of every size and style in every part of the country and in several other places in the world. I believe so much in what the church is and does that I can't seem to think of retiring.

With all of that, I have to admit that the church has often failed. I confess readily that we sometimes don't deserve the name we bear, the name of Jesus Christ. The great nineteenth-century novelist Herman Melville said that the pulpit of the church is "this earth's foremost part; all the rest comes in its rear; the pulpit leads the world."[1] Ideally, Melville was right. The pulpit ought to lead the way, breaking through the darkness of our world's journey and pointing to a land of promise. But in truth, the church sometimes defends what is wrong or speaks so cautiously about what is right that her voice is lost in the maelstrom of petty, passing ideas.

## Introducing Frederick Douglass

That's the pain that pesters me when I think of Frederick Douglass. I wish the church had more surely and vigorously done her job. I wish the church could lay a better claim to Frederick Douglass, but...well, let me tell you his story.

As far as he could estimate, Frederick Douglass was born sometime in 1818, the son of a slave woman, Harriet Bailey, and a white man, a slave owner. He had only fleeting memories of his mother. She was able to see him only by walking several miles at night after a day's work in the field of a nearby farmer. Later in his life, Douglass remembered his mother calling him her little valentine, which made him think he might have been born on February 14; but, as he often observed, most slaves knew as little of their birth date as horses knew of theirs.

When Douglass was seven or eight years old, he was transferred to a family in Baltimore. At first the wife showed great kindness to him and began teaching him to read. When her husband learned of this, however, he forbade any further teaching. In many places it was against the law to teach a slave to read because the ability to read would make slaves restless and rebellious. The boy's appetite for learning was insatiable, however, so he sought out every possible means of adding to his knowledge, often at the price of beatings. By a variety of subterfuges he also learned how to write. Often Douglass saw his learning as a curse rather than a blessing. It taught him, he said, to recognize his "wretched condition without the remedy. In moment of agony I envied my fellow-slaves for their stupidity. I...often wished myself a beast."[2]

Next to my relationship with God and the blessing of love and human friendship, I know of nothing I prize more than education. But I have discovered over the years that education isn't that priceless to everyone. Some seem to have little interest in learning, and others seem content to discontinue learning rather early in life. One wonders what drives some people to learn more and more, especially when the odds are seriously against them. So too, with the desire to better oneself. The slave boy, Frederick Bailey, somehow had this passion for learning and an insistence on bettering himself. Perhaps the passion and the insistence were there because his potential was so great. Certainly, when the door of opportunity opened for him, he was ready to walk through it. This strikes me as only a little short of a miracle.

Frederick trained himself and awaited his opportunity. At last he set a date for his escape from slavery: September 3, 1838, when he would have been, by best estimate, twenty-years-old. He was cautious during much of his lifetime about giving the details of his escape, for fear of implicating others. As he wrote later, his motto was, "Trust no man!" "I saw in every white man an enemy, and in almost every colored man cause for distrust."[3]

If this seems a bitter rule by which to live, one has to consider that Frederick knew his very life was at stake. In the culture of the slave world, he was a valuable commodity, worth hundreds of dollars. He knew by several years of observation that persons of either race might betray him for the dollars involved. If they did so, they could justify their actions by the law of the land. After all, a slave was by definition a piece of property with no rights of his or her own. To flee, therefore, was to "steal" oneself from the owner. Those who prevented the stealing were helping to enforce the law.

## Frederick Douglass the Escaped Slave

Yet Frederick made his escape! Because he was intelligent, a skilled laborer, and a hard worker, he was soon able to establish himself. Nevertheless, he had to live each day with the fear he might be apprehended and returned to his owner. He married a free slave, Anna Murray—described as "a plain dark woman, inclined toward stoutness and accustomed to wearing a bandanna handkerchief about her head."[4] She had no inclination to learning and never learned to read or write. In many ways she seemed a strange mate for Frederick, a commanding figure, a born leader, with elements of genius.

Frederick Augustus Washington Bailey changed his name to Frederick Douglass. He sought, as did most escaped slaves, to gain with a name-change a measure of protection against being returned to slavery. For three years he worked: first at odd jobs, then in a foundry, supporting Anna and his growing family. But his heart had been captured by the anti-slavery movement.

## Frederick Douglass's Anti-slavery Activities

One evening in 1841 he was asked to speak extemporaneously to an anti-slavery meeting. He so captured the audience that a whole new career opened before him. The Massachusetts Anti-Slavery Society asked him to work full time as a speaker, a fund raiser, and as dramatic evidence that a Negro was in no way of less worth than a white person.

Indeed, Frederick began to demonstrate this fact so well that white abolitionists sometimes urged him to modify his style, to sound more "plantation." His most powerful presentations, from a fund-raising point of view, were his stories of slave life as he had seen and experienced it. But he wanted more and more to deal with the philosophy of freedom and equality. His reasoning was so clear and his manner of speaking so effective that some listeners were sure he had never been a slave or that he was not really a Negro.

Douglass lectured widely through the north, electrifying crowds by his eloquence, his occasional barbs of mimicry, his commanding presence, and his innate dignity. Nevertheless, he knew he was always in danger of being taken by a bounty hunter, all the more so after publishing his book, *Narrative of the Life of Frederick Douglass,* in 1845.

Later that year he accepted an invitation to lecture in England and Ireland. There he became even more of a celebrity. England had abolished slavery a generation earlier, so Douglass found much support among the British for America to do the same. He enjoyed a level of freedom in his travels in England and Ireland that he had never known in America. It was not only that he had no fear of being apprehended but also that he was experiencing true equality for the first time. He heard no arguments about where he must travel or where he must stay. Almost from the beginning Douglass had envisioned freedom in this way, for nothing in his temperament would accept a segregated lifestyle. He believed a human being was a human being and should be treated as such.

## Frederick Douglass the Free Man

As time went by, British enthusiasm took on practical proportions in two particular ways. First, a group of friends raised seven hundred dollars to buy freedom for Frederick Douglass. That legal paper meant a great deal. Second, recognizing Douglass's ability with words, some of his supporters urged him to begin a newspaper in America with their financial underwriting.

This presented a problem. It meant going against the wishes of Douglass's hero and mentor, William Lloyd Garrison. Eventually, Douglass did so. For more than thirteen years he published a paper, known first as *The North Star* and later as *Frederick Douglass' Weekly*. Its circulation was never large. However, its influence was quite great, because major daily newspapers quoted him so frequently. His newspaper also offered a base of pride for the African American population.

## Frederick Douglass and the Approaching Showdown

As America moved ever closer to a showdown on the race question, Douglass's role became increasingly important. John Brown sought his support. While Douglass harbored no doubts about Brown's integrity and commitment, he felt that insurrection was not the course to follow. With the election of Abraham Lincoln, a still larger platform of influence opened for Douglass. Frederick Douglass decided during his first meeting with President Lincoln that the president was a person he could trust. No one can say with certainty what role Douglass might have played if President Lincoln had lived. Clearly the two men developed a level of respect that would have made their united efforts particularly effective.

Under succeeding national administrations, Frederick Douglass became for five years the Recorder of Deeds for the District of Columbia and for two years the U.S. Minister and Consul General to Haiti. Beyond all of that, he stood as a symbol to his own race of the rise from slavery. It was generally agreed that in his later years he was, next to the president and the vice-president, the best-known name in Washington, D.C. He had the inner dignity to suffer slight or delay without losing stature and the integrity to receive honor without sacrificing the cause of his people to his own preferment.

## Frederick Douglass a Source of Pain

As I indicated at the very outset, one thing about the Frederick Douglass story gives me pain. I wish he had felt tied to the church by affection and regard. Unfortunately, he had seen levels of hypocrisy that aroused nothing but bitterness. He would have classified many professing Christians with the scribes and Pharisees of whom Jesus said, "[D]o whatever they teach you and follow it; but do not do as they do, for they do not practice what they teach" (Mt. 23:3). Douglass recalled that his one-time owner had "attended a Methodist camp-meeting and there experienced religion. If it had any effect on his character, it made him more cruel and hateful in all his ways." How? Because with his conversion "he found religious sanction and support for his slaveholding cruelty."[5]

Douglass employed all his eloquence to express his anger. "We have men-stealers for ministers, women-whippers for missionaries, and cradle-plunderers for church members," he wrote. "The slave auctioneer's bell and the church-going bell chime in with each other, and the bitter cries of the heart-broken slave are drowned in the religious shouts of his pious master." As he described the inconsistencies of church members, Douglass picked up the words of Jesus in Matthew 23:24. "'They strain at a gnat and swallow a camel' [KJV]...They would be shocked at the proposition of fellowshipping a *sheep*-stealer; and at the same time they hug to their communion a *man*-stealer, and brand me an infidel if I find fault with them for it."[6]

Frederick Douglass knew the difference, and he expressed that difference with the same vigorous language. "What I have said respecting and against religion, I mean strictly to apply to the *slaveholding religion* of this land, and with no possible reference to Christianity proper; for between the Christianity of this land, and the Christianity of Christ, I recognize the widest possible difference—so wide, that to receive the one as good, pure, and holy is of necessity to reject the other as bad, corrupt, and wicked....I love the pure, peaceable, and impartial Christianity of Christ: I therefore hate the corrupt, slaveholding, women-whipping, cradle-plundering, partial and hypocritical Christianity of this land."[7]

Douglass's language is reminiscent of our Lord's when he cried, "Woe to you, scribes and Pharisees, hypocrites!" (Mt. 23:23). I can't refute what Douglass charged. I am cautious about passing judgment on other generations, because all of us live rather much within the light of our times and find it difficult to see beyond that light. I don't believe I could ever accept the idea of slavery, but I say that from the safe boundaries of the twenty-first century.

Of this I am very sure: even if one could accept, in another time, the philosophical idea of slavery, one can never justify the physical abuse of other persons. I think this is something of what the apostle Paul is saying when he makes no comment about slavery as a system, but insists, "Masters, treat your slaves justly and fairly, for you know that you also have a Master in heaven" (Col. 4:1). Before God, Paul insisted, "there is no longer...slave and free; but Christ is all and in all!" (Col. 3:11).

Of course another question arises. Why didn't Frederick Douglass follow a less angry road, like Richard Allen, another former slave, who founded the African Methodist Episcopal Church? Or the noted slave preacher, Father Jasper, who moved both whites and blacks by his preaching? I must again answer, with honesty and humility, that I don't know. Again I do not feel justified in passing judgment on what these men, in another generation, chose to do.

Of one thing I am sure, however, indeed, of two. First, you and I are responsible under God to seek to be Christlike in our time and in our place. Beyond that we are responsible to be sensitive to the fact that some future generation may judge us as hypocritical in our handling of some human problem as Douglass rightly judged the slave owners of his day. This is to say, we need a great deal of humility and wonderfully open hearts and minds if we are to be the Christians we ought to be. That is, if we are to live up to our name.

CHAPTER 12

# Susan B. Anthony
*The Woman Who Made Reform
an Active Verb*

Now that women constitute a solid minority and sometimes a slight majority in graduate schools of law, medicine, and theology, you might reckon that the feminist story is being adequately told. Not so. As any movement begins to come into its own, the pioneers of the movement are likely to be forgotten, or even more likely to be awaiting discovery. Students of a movement or students of a particular period of history may well know some of these names and personalities, but the general public does not.

## Introducing Susan B. Anthony

Such stories ought to be told. It's not only a matter of fairness and not only a matter of knowing one's ideological roots, but it's also the issue of knowing our ancestors so we can really know ourselves. So it is that we look at Susan B. Anthony, one of our bona fide ancestors who was a part of most of the significant sociological and religious movements of the nineteenth century. She was a true pioneer in the early struggle for women's rights.

### Basic Background

Susan Brownell Anthony was born in South Adams, Massachusetts, in 1820. True to her vigorous Quaker heritage, she was one of the early abolitionists and worked passionately in the fight against slavery. But this was only one of Miss Anthony's commitments. As a school teacher, she called for equal pay for women teachers; she was a leader in the temperance crusade; and she lectured and exhorted from the public platform when few women dared do so. For two years, she and Elizabeth Cady Stanton published a weekly newspaper, *The Revolution*. She was one of the authors of the four-volume work, *The History of Woman Suffrage*. She died in 1906 thirteen years before the nineteenth amendment to the Constitution granted women the full right to vote.

## Communities of Interest

Susan Anthony's story appeals to anyone who is interested in equal human rights, and particularly to those with convictions about the rights of women and of ethnic minorities. Her story is also interesting to the advocates of equal pay for comparable work. Miss Anthony's sense of independence and her readiness to go to battle wherever she saw injustice makes her fascinating to anyone who enjoys meeting folks who march to their own drummer, but who do so with style and a measure of eventual effectiveness. Her story can be told with particular appropriateness on Martin Luther King Sunday, on Labor Day Sunday, or on a Sunday that celebrates women's role in the church. If her story is told on the Sunday before Election Day, it may goad some lazy citizens to reassert their right to vote.

## SERMON

# Susan B. Anthony:
## The Woman Who Made Reform an Active Verb

### Scripture Lesson: James 2:14–26

Some people don't get the notice they deserve. That's painfully clear in our contemporary society, where the literature of the checkout counter seems to major in those who have the best press agents or those who win attention for the most unsavory reasons. It's true in the history books, too—especially true for those persons who pioneer for great causes but die without seeing their causes triumph. Often the latecomers to a movement forget they stand on shoulders.

## Susan B. Anthony's Background

So let me tell you about Susan Brownell Anthony. I've described her as "the woman who made 'reform' an active verb." Let me hasten to comfort all of you grammarians. I know that "reform" is an active verb from a grammatical point of view. I'm speaking just now from a philosophical point of view. Many persons who believe in the need for change never get around to making a difference; indeed, that may include most of us. We believe in reform, but nothing seems to come of our believing.

Susan Anthony doesn't belong in such company. For her, reform was something that made one write, speak, legislate, march, and if necessary, get arrested. *Reform* for her, was an active verb. She didn't just think it or believe in it. She labored to make it happen. As she herself put it, "I would rather *make* history than write it."[1]

Susan Anthony had a head start toward reform. She was born into what one biographer calls "a family of independent-minded Quakers." As one who admires the Quakers for their sense of social responsibility, I'm amused at the term, "independent-minded Quakers." I didn't know there was any other kind. It seems to me that a Quaker is by definition, of an independent mind. When the unnecessary adjective is added to the Quaker designation for Susan's family, you know they were people who took causes, inequities, and human needs seriously. *Very* seriously! This is the kind of home into which Susan Anthony was born, in 1820, in South Adams, Massachusetts. Her father was a man of moral zeal. Several of her women ancestors spoke out more vigorously than was expected or appreciated in their time. Susan quickly proved her right to a place on such a family tree.

## Susan B. Anthony the Reformer

She was a schoolteacher for fifteen years, but she made waves within her profession, campaigning for equal pay for women teachers. This theme later became a dominant note in her whole feminist philosophy. She was convinced that women could never enjoy true equality unless they had independent economic strength. She raised her voice in 1853, and in years following, at the New York State Teacher's Convention to call for equality in education for women and for blacks. She was a woman of conviction, and she seemed never to keep those convictions a secret.

Also in the early 1850s, she became involved in the temperance movement. Abolition, temperance, and women's rights were often interlocking causes at that time, drawing on much of the same leadership. Temperance and women's rights continued to be a common enterprise into the twentieth century. Susan tried to speak at a Sons of Temperance meeting, but was refused the floor. She then organized the Women's State Temperance Society of New York. Following the style of her parents, she became increasingly active in the abolitionist movement, serving from 1856 to 1861 as an agent of the American Anti-Slavery Society. In her diary she spoke of William Lloyd Garrison, the most vigorous abolitionist, as the "most Christ-like man" she had ever known.[2]

## Susan B. Anthony and Women's Rights

Despite Anthony's passion for a variety of causes, everything ranked second to her commitment to the rights of women. She felt it was "the cause of causes" because it was the "principle underlying" all other reform. She insisted that the Fourteenth and Fifteenth Amendments to the Constitution, providing for the enfranchisement of the former slaves, should also include the right for women to vote. When it did not do so, she argued that the way had been left open for every kind of injustice to "other and weaker men and peoples." Susan knew how to turn a neat phrase. She would have done well in our sound-byte culture. At this point in her case she said, "Men who fail to be just to their mothers cannot be expected to be just to each other."[3] You might argue with her logic and question her syllogism, but it would be hard to get past the emotional shock of her statement.

She was by no means alone in her conviction about the primary importance of woman's suffrage. All the leaders of the suffrage movement worked with the same basic conviction: their movement would lead the way to every other kind of worthy reform. The other leaders tended to emphasize the moral quality of women and thus the conscience they would bring to the ballot box. Anthony seemed more to build her argument on the issue of fairness and the logic that would flow from it. If women could not be treated as equal members of the human race, how could one expect other persons–the poor, the immigrant, the intellectually or physically disadvantaged–to have a fair hearing?

## Susan B. Anthony and the Working Woman

A key issue, as I said earlier, was economics. She learned during her work with the temperance cause that unless women had money, they couldn't bring reform to pass. Their hearts might be in the right place, but someone would have to pay the bills. She referred to women's economic position as "the bread of dependence," insisting that women would always be degraded if they had to depend on someone else for their sustenance. She was fighting a complicated battle. She said that women were "in chains" (picking up the language of abolitionism), but that–the more debasing!–"they do not realize it." Again, in the language of abolition, she said in 1869, "Still another form of slavery remains to be disposed of; the old idea yet prevails that woman is owned and possessed by man, to be clothed and fed and cared for by his generosity."[4]

This may be one reason why Ms. Anthony gave increasing attention to working women. The woman living in comfortable middle class or upper middle class circumstances wouldn't find as much appeal in Ms. Anthony's argument. She urged the one hundred thousand women school teachers to seek the ballot and thus double their salaries. She pointed to statistics indicating that three million women in America were supporting themselves, most of them in the lowliest forms of work. Over 50,000 received less than fifty cents a day, she said. I'm sure she would be thrilled to see the increasing percentage of women in professional and executive positions today, but she might be all the more frustrated to find that, a century after her campaigning, a significant gap in comparative income remains.

## The Unbending Susan B. Anthony

There was little bending in Susan B. Anthony. The traditional proverb advises us to "choose the lesser of two evils." She said, "Of two evils, choose neither." Even those who work in great causes sometimes find themselves in situations where they must weigh the consequences of their actions. What if taking a strong stand alienates a possible constituency, for instance? Anthony's answer was always the same: "Do right, and leave the consequences to God."

Others have second-guessed her on some of these decisions. She decided to challenge the law on Election Day, 1872. She and other suffragists believed the Fourteenth and Fifteenth Amendments could be interpreted as allowing women to vote. Susan and some supporters and a few others across the country went to vote. She was arrested and brought to trial. She challenged the judge, saying that every person dealing with her case was her "political sovereign," since she had no right to vote: "native or foreign, white or black, rich or poor, educated or ignorant, wake or asleep, sober or drunk, each and every man of them was my political superior; hence, in no sense, my peer." Jury, judge, and counsel, she said, were all of a "superior class" to her.[5]

No matter! The Court found her guilty and fined her one hundred dollars and the costs of prosecution. Susan promptly announced that she would not pay the fine. Because she would not pay the fine, neither could the case be appealed. A different kind of personality would have acquiesced to the fine to pursue the matter in the courts of the land. Would that have been better? Perhaps. But we would have lost Susan's dramatic declaration, including her grand sentence, "Resistance to tyranny is obedience to God."

When I read that line, I remember my sixth grade Sunday school teacher who had our class of boys memorize, "Then Peter and the other apostles answered and said, We ought to obey God rather than men" (Acts 5:29, KJV). I wonder if any of that rhythm or philosophy was in Susan Anthony's mind when she spoke her piece.

## Susan B. Anthony's Religion

She knew her Bible, no doubt about that. Her writings, both formal and personal, are filled with allusions and figures of speech from the scriptures. But she didn't belong to the evangelical branch that was so often prominent in the abolition, temperance, and suffrage movements. True to her particular Quaker heritage, she placed more faith in the inner light than in institutional structures. As for the scriptures, she was offended that so many of her opponents in issues of both slavery and women's rights had used the scriptures to make their points. She said, with understandable asperity, that she thought women had as good a right to interpret and twist the Bible to their own advantage, as men had always twisted it to theirs. She had little sympathy with those who argued for the plenary inspiration of the Bible, although no doubt a great many of her loyal followers were in that number.

If Paul's epistles teach something different from the Epistle of James, as scholars and common folk have argued off and on through the centuries, Susan Anthony came down hard on James's side, whether she ever said so or not. Paul worked hard in defining the doctrines of the church. Susan had little interest in doctrine. Clearly sometimes it got in her way. For her, the issue was work. She wouldn't by any means have classified it by the theological term, "works righteousness," because she didn't claim any righteousness for what she was doing. It's just that she measured Christianity by what it did. This was her reason for finding godliness in William Lloyd Garrison, because he put his convictions into action.

James wrote, "What good is it, my brothers and sisters, if you say you have faith but do not have works? Can faith save you? If a brother or sister is naked and lacks daily food, and one of you says to them, 'Go in peace; keep warm and eat your fill,' and yet you do not supply their bodily needs, what is the good of that? So faith by itself, if it has no works, is dead" (Jas. 2:14–17). Susan Anthony could buy that. For her, that was pretty much the whole package. So she would say, "I pray every single second of my life; not on my knees but with my work."[6]

## Susan B. Anthony and Marriage

At one point, believe it or not, Susan was in company with the apostle Paul. Both of them had an extraordinary sense of the urgency of their work, a sense so strong that it influenced their attitudes toward marriage. Paul wrote the people at Corinth that "in view of the impending crisis," they should be cautious about marriage; he had noticed that "the married man is anxious about the affairs of the world, how to please his wife," while the unmarried concentrated on the work of the Lord (1 Cor. 7:26–35). Ms. Anthony operated on the same principle. She was said to have had many male admirers, but she left no time for romance. For her, there was always work to be done. She discouraged marriage among the young suffragists. Her objection was that women threw away every other purpose in their lives to conform themselves to the wishes of men. For her, there was always work to be done, and that governed the day.

I suspect that most of us, if we think of heaven, shape it somewhat according to our personalities. One of my mother's favorite songs spoke about taking a "vacation in heaven." That was a pretty attractive idea to my parents. My father worked a six-day week all his life. He didn't get a paid vacation (a week) until he was in his sixties, so I empathize with my mother's love of a vacation in heaven. In the same way I empathize with the persons who first sang of heaven as a place where they would put on their shoes and put on their robe, so they could "walk all over God's heaven." People who never had shoes or a robe saw that as a symbol of God's new victory in their lives.

For Susan Anthony, heaven had better be a place of activity. As she wrote to her longtime co-worker, Elizabeth Cady Stanton, "Oh the world is so full of work for those who work at all–I see no old fashioned *heaven* for me–to sit and sing and glorify." Indeed, if she got to "the other life" while women were still without the franchise, the glories of heaven wouldn't interest her as much as the work for women on earth.

## The Legacy of Susan B. Anthony

So Susan Anthony was no doubt at home with everything James said. She had a passionate energy for the things she believed in, and she was nearly tireless in pursuing those convictions. While she placed herself at odds with those who made much of doctrine, she was unflinchingly doctrinaire about what she believed. Hers may not have been the conventional doctrines of the church, but she treated her opinions with as much vigor and defensiveness as did any professional theologian. The point above all others, as far as she was concerned, was that our deeds should be consistent with our stated beliefs. Indeed, those deeds are the only significant measure of our Christianity.

She maintained her passion to the end. When some men publicly praised her on her eighty-fifth birthday, she replied that women didn't need men's compliments or their worship unless men also recognized women's right to justice. In her last public address before her death in 1906, she paid tribute to the women who had led the way in the struggle for the rights of women. She regretted that she could not name every one, and then continued, "but with such women consecrating their lives...failure is impossible."

She could see the land of promise, and she was confident that work would win it.

# CHAPTER 13

# Fanny J. Crosby

## She Set the World to Singing

Let me venture an extravagant statement. I can't prove it, but I throw it out for your consideration. I submit that one of the most influential theologians of the late nineteenth and early twentieth centuries is Fanny Crosby. Further, I submit that she is quoted more by the person in the pews than any other theologian you or I might name. Still further, if our thinking has any affective elements, Fanny Crosby may outdistance her rivals beyond measure because her theology comes to us in an affective form by way of hymns.

### Introducing Fanny J. Crosby

Over a century ago, a wise observer of the human scene said, "Give me the making of the songs of a nation, and I care not who makes its laws."[1] By the same measure, and perhaps more emphatically, the songs church folk sing, whether at worship or at home, go farther in shaping their theology than do the classes in which they are taught or (as a longtime pastor, I hate to say it) the sermons they hear. John Wesley made peace with this fact of the comparative power of sermon and hymn to communicate theology. Thus he could refer to the collection of the hymns of his brother Charles as "a little body of divinity." Of course, John exercised some editorial control over Charles's hymns.

The fact remains, however, that the hymns of Fanny J. Crosby have been a powerful element in shaping the thinking of the average person in the pews. They have inspired dedication, given a vehicle for praise, and comforted persons in distress. All this from a woman who was blind for all but the first six weeks of her long life.

### Basic Background

Fanny Jane Crosby was born March 24, 1820, in the town of Southeast, New York, to John and Marcy Crosby. When she was six weeks old and afflicted with an inflammation of the eyes, an itinerant doctor gave a remedy that left her permanently blind. She possessed a remarkably retentive mind. By the time she was ten or eleven, she could recite the Pentateuch, the four gospels, many Psalms, all of Proverbs, all of Ruth and the Song of Solomon from memory. She began writing poetry when she was no more than eight years old but didn't write her first hymn until she was in her forties. Although she married Alexander Van Alstyne in 1858, even in her own lifetime she was always known as "Mrs. Crosby" or simply as Fanny Crosby.

At the height of her creativity she was writing so many hymns that they were published under 204 pen names. In total, she wrote more than 8,000 hymns. By the time she died in 1915, just short of her ninety-fifth birthday, she was one of the best known women in America.

### Communities of Interest

Fanny Crosby has particular appeal to people who love familiar hymns. In many instances even these people will be surprised to learn that the hymns they love came from this person. She appeals also to those who honor persons for rising above their difficulties, who have to cope with some sort of physical, emotional, social, or educational challenge.

I have told Fanny Crosby's story a number of times in a variety of settings, but I have never done so in the structure of a sermon. This material is somewhat more condensed than what I have used in lecture settings. Obviously a service telling Fanny Crosby's story should include several of her hymns.

## SERMON _____

# Fanny J. Crosby: *She Set the World to Singing*

## Scripture Lesson: John 9:1–7, 38–41

I want to tell you the story of a remarkable woman. She lived through most of the nineteenth century and well into the twentieth and set the world to singing. To lead us into her story properly, I need to remind us of a story from the gospel of John. One day Jesus and his disciples came upon a man who had been blind from birth. Jesus proceeded to heal him, but the miracle of the healing isn't the end of the story. The man soon found himself in a theological discussion with some religious leaders of the day, persons who were enemies of Jesus. These leaders essentially excommunicated the man, after which the man acknowledged Jesus as his Lord, worshiping him.

Jesus then said a remarkable thing. "I came into this world for judgment so that those who do not see may see, and those who do see may become blind" (Jn. 9:39). Jesus' enemies sensed that the words were directed at them and answered him, "Surely we are not blind, are we?" Jesus answered, still more sharply, "If you were blind, you would not have sin. But now that you say, 'We see,' your sin remains" (Jn. 9:40–41). Jesus was saying that you may be blind in two ways. I suspect it's clear that while physical blindness is one of the saddest limitations that can come to a human life, it is not even to be compared to spiritual blindness.

## Introducing Fanny J. Crosby

Fanny J. Crosby, the woman whose story I want to tell, was only six weeks old when her eyes became seriously inflamed. Her worried parents consulted an itinerant who claimed to be a doctor. Over the objection of her parents, he put burning hot poultices on the infant's eyes to draw out the infection. The infection gradually left, but Fanny was left blind except for a slight perception of light. She lived with this physical blindness through all of her nearly ninety-five years, but I submit that few people on our planet have ever had better spiritual sight than did Fanny Crosby.

If you had been Fanny's mother, Marcy, you might have felt that God and fate were conspiring against you. Not only had erratic treatment blinded her little girl, but then her husband, John, died of flu or pneumonia only a short time later, when Fanny was not yet eight months old.

A special kind of redemption was soon at work by way of Fanny's grandmother, Eunice. She resolved that Fanny would not be handicapped by her blindness. Years later Fanny recalled that though she never knew what it was to see with her eyes, at six she could "climb a tree like a squirrel and ride a horse bareback." Still more important, Eunice communicated her faith to Fanny. Every Sunday they walked barefoot to church, shoes in hand. At age eight, Fanny put her feelings on paper, in what may have been her first poem:

Oh, what a happy child I am,
Although I CANNOT SEE!
I am resolved that in this world
Contented I will be!
How many blessings I enjoy
That other people don't!
So weep or sigh became I'm blind,
I cannot–nor I won't.

I can't claim such an admirably positive outlook, but it's a mindset I cherish. It's very clear that whatever physical sight Fanny Crosby lacked, she was superb in her spiritual vision.

When Fanny was eight or nine, she and her mother moved. Fanny then came under the influence of Mrs. Hawley, their landlady. This devout woman saw the potential of Fanny's bright mind and began teaching her to memorize. Within two years, Fanny could recite the Pentateuch, the four gospels, Ruth, Song of Solomon, and many of the Psalms. No wonder, she would say in her later years that the Bible had nurtured her through all her life, and no wonder that her hymns drew so easily on biblical insights and figures of speech.

As a child, she was fiercely competitive. She wanted no concessions for her blindness. When she was nearly 15, she enrolled in the New York Institution for the Blind for the beginning of her very brief formal education. Her poetry made a place for her in the school. When the poet and newspaper editor, William Cullen Bryant, visited the school, he praised her work.

This was a time when poetry belonged to the people in a way that it has not in the past generation or two. Poetry was read at nearly every public occasion, and almost anyone was likely to try putting thoughts in verse. Probably much of what was written and read was hardly more than simple rhyming, but it provided an appreciation for the gift and a setting that encouraged a talent like Fanny's.

## Fanny J. Crosby's Religious Experiences

Although Fanny had grown up in a pious atmosphere and knew the scriptures so well, she was thirty years old before she felt satisfied that her heart was related to God as she wanted it to be. It happened on November 20, 1850, during revival services at the Broadway Tabernacle in New York City. She explained, "My very soul was flooded with celestial light."

In 1864, when Fanny was turning forty-four, she had a vision of heaven and with it a call to write religious music. She had been writing poetry all her life, but she had never written a hymn. This is hard to understand, in light of Fanny's knowledge of the scriptures and her strong personal faith. I'm sure there's some sort of lesson here for all of us: are we missing the relationship between our gifts and our opportunities to serve God? She teamed up with William Bradbury, a well-established composer, music publisher, and piano manufacturer. However, Bradbury died less than four years later. As Fanny filed by his casket, devastated by the loss and feeling that Bradbury's death had taken her new form of ministry from her, she heard a mysterious voice: "Fanny, pick up the work where Bradbury has left it. Take your harp from the willow, and dry your tears." Others heard the voice, but couldn't identify the source. For Fanny, it was a divine mandate.

## Fanny J. Crosby's Hymn Writing

Before long, a Cincinnati business tycoon, Howard Doane, sought out Fanny. He loved to write music. His tunes were simple, the kind Fanny felt were best. Without records or radio, the more easily a tune could be picked up the better. Doane wrote that kind of tune. On one occasion, he stopped by Fanny's modest New York flat and told her that he had just forty minutes before he had to catch a train for Cincinnati, but he wanted Fanny to hear a tune he had just composed. When she heard it, she clapped her hands, as she always did when something pleased her. "Why, that says, 'Safe in the arms of Jesus,'" she said. She excused herself, withdrew to the other room of her apartment, and within half an hour had completed the hymn.

Fanny's remarkable memory was essential to her work, since she was unable to write. She was in her eighties before she learned to write her name, which she did to satisfy people who wanted her autograph.

William Doane and Fanny collaborated on a number of hymns, including "Pass Me Not, O Gentle Savior," "I Am Thine, O Lord," and "Rescue the Perishing." The latter became the unofficial theme song of the home missions movement of American Protestantism. Doane asked Fanny to speak for a group of Cincinnati workingmen. Fanny had a strong feeling that some boy in the crowd had forsaken his mother's faith, and she said so. Perhaps this is another instance where Fanny's lack of physical vision made her more open to what some would call "intuition" and what others would call "the leading of the Holy Spirit." In any event, Fanny followed her sense. When she finished her talk, an eighteen-year-old came forward to accept Christ and to return to the faith of his home. That night, Fanny couldn't fall asleep for thinking of a phrase Doane had given her in connection with the evening's assignment: "Rescue the Perishing." Before falling asleep, she wrote the hymn.

## The Simplicity of Fanny J. Crosby

Fanny possessed a fine mind. She was capable of writing rather good poetry and music, but she was dedicated to making her work as accessible as possible to as many people as possible. Now and again while looking at her hymns one recognizes the depth below the apparently simple phrases. Consider the theology of mission in a verse from "Rescue the Perishing":

> Down in the human heart, crushed by the tempter,
> Feelings lie buried that grace can restore;
> Touched by a loving heart, wakened by kindness,
> Chords that were broken will vibrate once more.[2]

It is not great poetry, but it's more than simple rhyming. There is structure, a plot line, an engaging rhythm, a feeling for human beings, and above all, a passion. Fanny wrote from a sense of calling.

As a result, she worried not at all about the benefits she might accrue. As I indicated earlier, William Doane was a very successful businessman, who was also admirably generous in his support of charitable institutions. Another of Fanny's collaborators was Phoebe Knapp, whose husband founded the Metropolitan Life Insurance Company. With Phoebe Knapp, Fanny wrote what is probably her best known hymn, "Blessed Assurance." Fanny was a frequent guest in these luxurious homes, yet she chose to live in a tenement apartment.

## Fanny J. Crosby's Passion

Fanny lived during a period of evangelical fervor in America, much of it nurtured by popular hymns. Two publishing houses that produced hymn collections at regular intervals engaged Fanny's services. Hugh Main, her major publisher, would sometimes say that he needed twenty selections for an Easter collection, and Fanny would go to work on them. She was usually paid only a dollar or two for each poem. Many of her friends felt the publishers exploited her. Fanny didn't see it that way. She was simply doing a favor for her friends. She felt that her reward was in the persons who were led to God by what she had written.

As for the money, she tended to give it away. Sometimes this prodigal generosity became an occasion for the mysterious and wonderful. One day in 1874, she didn't know how she would pay her rent. With no resources, she began to pray. A man whom she had never met appeared at her door. He left as quickly as he had come, after pressing a ten-dollar bill in her hand–exactly the amount she needed to pay her rent. Out of that experience, she wrote the words to the hymn, "All the Way My Savior Leads Me." Fanny thought of a hymn as "a song of the heart addressed to God." In some instances, her definition had a pretty existential quality. Although so many hundreds of her hymns were written on assignment, with no occasion for particular inspiration, she saw even these routine projects as part of her communion with God.

As she entered her sixties, Fanny came to feel that her major responsibility was as a home mission worker. This broad term covered such ministries as rescue missions, work in the slums, services for the workers at factories, shops, and street meetings–in truth, wherever one might find human need. She felt this was the most wonderful work in the world because it provided such an opportunity to love people.

Love was Fanny's hallmark. As time went by, she was invited more and more often to speak in churches. She always began the same way, "God bless your dear hearts, I'm so happy to be with you!"

Perhaps her physical blindness assisted her mission of love. Others might be turned off by people's clothing or personal appearance, but Fanny had no such barrier. With her blindness, she didn't allow her own appearance to get in her way. She was four feet nine inches tall, with what is usually described as a "horse" face, prominent, gapped front teeth, jug ears, and of course dark glasses. But no one could doubt that she walked, talked, and lived with love.

## Fanny J. Crosby's Greatest Favor

She had such extraordinary vision! Now and again people spoke accusingly of the doctor whose treatment had blinded her, but Fanny would answer, "Don't blame the doctor. If I could meet him, I would tell him that he unwittingly did me the greatest favor in the world." She felt that sight might have been a distraction to her. She reasoned that her powers of concentration came from her blindness as did her extraordinary memory.

## Fanny J. Crosby's Legacy

Fanny's ninety-third birthday came on Easter. She said, "If there is anyone in this world happier than I, I want to shake his hand, for I believe myself to be as happy as it is possible for a mortal to be in this world."[3] When she died, nearly two years later, her funeral was said to have been the largest ever seen in Bridgeport, larger even than that of P. T. Barnum.

For forty years the marker on her grave said only, "Aunt Fanny. She hath done what she could." In 1955, however, the citizens of Bridgeport raised up a large marble slab with more of her story, including the first verse of "Blessed Assurance." They might well have added the line, "She saw what too many of us miss."

CHAPTER 14

# Emily Dickinson
## *Cautious Seeker*

William Bowers, an assistant professor of English literature in a Florida community college, confesses that it's a struggle to convey a love of literature in those who are better acquainted with Jerry Springer or Hulk Hogan. He quotes a student as saying, "Seems like all we read in here is freaks."[1]

### Introducing Emily Dickinson

I wasn't surprised to find that one of the authors covered in Dr. Bowers's course is Emily Dickinson. We might easily conclude that Emily Dickinson was a bit of a freak, especially if we measure life exclusively by a postmodern sensate standard. Except for a year of study in her late teens, Emily Dickinson almost never left her hometown of Amherst, Massachusetts. Indeed, in the last twenty years of her life, she left the grounds of her home only once. She chose to be a recluse, while roaming the universe with her poetry and her letters. In all this roaming, God and immortality were constant points of issue. Some people are fascinating for the outward issues of their lives, their round of activities. Emily Dickinson fascinates us by her interior journeys, the endless quest of solitude.

### Basic Background

Emily Dickinson was born December 10, 1830, in Amherst, Massachusetts, where her father was an honored community leader. From 1840–47 she was a student at Amherst Academy. She then spent a year at Mount Holyoke Female Seminary. In 1850 a religious revival swept Amherst and became a significant issue in Emily's life. From 1858–1865, she wrote more than one thousand poems, more than half of her lifetime production. Miss Dickinson died on May 15, 1886. The first edition of her *Poems* was published in November, 1890, while the first edition of *Letters of Emily Dickinson* was published in November, 1894.

### Communities of Interest

Emily Dickinson holds special appeal to those who love literature. Two scholarly organs, *Dickinson Studies* and *The Emily Dickinson Journal,* indicate the depth of interest in her work, as does the constant flow of special pieces in journals and books or portions of books. She also has continuing appeal for those interested in women's studies and for persons who simply like anything related to New England, especially the literature of nineteenth-century New England. In "selling" the subject to a congregation, you may want to note that they have probably quoted Emily Dickinson without necessarily knowing it. She appears 21 times in *The Oxford Dictionary of Quotations,* and 71 times in The Seventeenth Edition of *Bartlett's Familiar Quotations.* I wonder how many times and places one has come upon her lines, "Success is counted sweetest / By those who ne'er succeed."

**SERMON** _____

# Emily Dickinson: *Cautious Seeker*

## Scripture Lesson: 2 Timothy 4:9–18

We preachers love to tell conversion stories. This is true regardless of our theology. For one, it's the story of a full-fledged sinner saved by grace. For another, the narrative may describe a war advocate who has now become a pacifist or a money-lover transformed into a person who tithes and more. Whatever the change, depending on the preacher, we love conversion stories.

Not everyone goes through such dramatic changes. Some who make such changes seem later to go back to their old ways. This has been true since the earliest days of the Christian faith.

Even the apostle Paul found it to be so. When he preached on Mars Hill, some "became believers," but "some scoffed" (Acts 17:32–34). Near the end of his ministry, Paul referred to one particularly sad case, Demas. At earlier times, Demas had been one of Paul's faithful assistants, the kind he probably referred to as "a promising young man." But now Demas "has deserted me," Paul writes, because he is "in love with this present world" (2 Tim. 4:9). A little farther along in this letter Paul sounds even more disappointed. "At my first defense no one came to my support, but all deserted me." He's gracious enough to add, "May it not be counted against them!" (2 Tim. 4:16) but the pathos is still there. Even for Paul, not everyone is converted; and even among those who are converted, not everyone holds on to the end.

## Emily Dickinson's Background

Well, I want to tell you the story of a very remarkable woman, Emily Dickinson. She walked on the edge of faith all her life, sometimes wonderfully affirming and sometimes drawing back. If a poet is to be known by his or her subject matter or if a person is to be judged by letters written to friends and family, very few people have been more conscious of God through a lifetime than Emily Dickinson. But she was always cautious. She sought, but with reticence. I'm certain she is like us—some of us all the time and most of us at passing times. Let me tell you her story.

Emily Dickinson was born December 10, 1830, in Amherst, Massachusetts. Her lawyer-father was a leading citizen of their community, serving as treasurer of Amherst College and as a United States congressman. Spiritually, Edward Dickinson was the kind of person many of us have known. He was earnest and disciplined enough to lead his family in evening prayers for many years, though he did not make a public confession of faith in Jesus Christ until he was forty-seven years old. I venture that many of the most beautiful Christians followed a course of conventional religion for a long time before registering a climactic moment. It isn't surprising that so many persons who come forward in Billy Graham meetings are longtime church members.

Meanwhile, Emily's soul was seeking its own way. As a fifteen-year-old, she confided in a letter to her closest friend, Abiah Root, that she had professed faith in Christ. "I felt I had found my savior. I never enjoyed such perfect peace and happiness."[2] She didn't say when this had happened or when it was that she lost this early ecstasy. The way of loss is the way many of us have known. She began to neglect her morning prayers until gradually "old habits returned" and her interest in religion diminished. But she added, "I feel that I shall never be happy without I love Christ."[3]

Not long before her seventeenth birthday, Emily entered Mount Holyoke Female Seminary. The term "seminary," which we now associate with a school for theological training, was used in those days to describe a secondary or higher level school for women. Life at Mount Holyoke was governed by more than seventy rules. The goal was a quality education, but to a purpose: its students would share in bringing the world to Christ. Mary Lyon, Mount Holyoke's founder, was still its head when Emily was a student.

## The Religious Struggles of Emily Dickinson

Lyon aimed to bring each of her students to a personal commitment to Christ. In Emily's year, 150 of the 230 students identified themselves as Christians by Miss Lyon's severe definition. About fifty were considered "hopers," persons who felt they were on the verge of conversion. Emily was classified with the thirty who were "without hope" because they were neither converted nor leaning strongly that way.

Well into that school year, Emily wrote Abiah Root that she had not yet made such a decision, but that she was "not entirely thoughtless on so important & serious a subject." But no decision was made. As Emily prepared to leave Mount Holyoke, she wrote Abiah that she regretted that she "did not give up and become a Christian." Why had she resisted? "[I]t is hard for me to give up the world."[4]

Emily's language reminds one of the apostle Paul's summary of Demas, who was "in love with this present world." The phrase sounds strange in Emily's mouth, when one considers that she retreated almost fully from the world in the last three decades of her life. But it reminds us that "the world" is a term variously defined by each of us. The world that keeps a quiet scholar from a faith commitment may seem like a monastery to a full-blown libertine. In truth, Emily found a vast world within her own mind, so that years later she would write a friend that she didn't need to travel, because "to shut our eyes is Travel." Emily's world was a very large one, and she felt she would have to give it up if she were to accept Christ as Lord.

Two years after Emily's return to Amherst, her town experienced a revival of religion. It was not marked by the kind of emotionalism seen in the Kentucky revivals of that period. Yet it was a powerful influence in the whole community, including Amherst College, but not for Emily, not even when her sister Lavinia, with whom she was very close, and her brother Austin, made their public decisions. In a letter to Jane Humphrey, Emily described the effect of the revival on some of her friends. "They seem so very tranquil, and their voices are kind, and gentle, and the tears fill their eyes so often, I really think I envy them."[5] Nevertheless, Emily did not follow their course. Call her a cautious seeker.

## Emily Dickinson the Poet

Emily began more and more to put her thoughts on paper. She produced what we now think of as some of the greatest poetry ever produced by an American author, but in Emily's own time her genius was never recognized. This was largely because Miss Dickinson herself kept her work hidden. On April 15, 1862, she sent four of her poems to Thomas Wentworth Higginson, in response to his article in *The Atlantic Monthly*. Thomas H. Johnson, a major Dickinson scholar, ranked this date with that of Ralph Waldo Emerson's Phi Beta Kappa address and Walt Whitman's first circulating of *Leaves of Grass* as three of the most significant dates in nineteenth-century American literary history.[6]

It seems somewhat ironic to give such significance to the beginning of correspondence with Higginson, since his counsel was that she should not try to publish. He saw the beauty of both her thoughts and her words but couldn't classify her work as poetry. Her form, her rhyme, and her metric beat were all unorthodox. She was charting a new course, and she continued for the rest of her life to chart it privately.

Higginson remained her literary confidant. When Dickinson died, Higginson worked with Mabel Loomis Todd to publish a selection of her poems. Even then he doubted public acceptance and altered some of the lines, meter, and language.

As it turned out, the publication in 1890 was very successful, so 166 more verses were published in a book the following year. The rest, as they say, is history. Although only seven of her poems were published during her lifetime, the entire body of her work—some 1,775 poems—are now bound in one volume and studied widely in college courses. Two scholarly journals are dedicated to her work, and evaluative and biographical books and articles continue to be published.

Merriam-Webster's *Dictionary of American Writers* describes her as "today universally regarded as one of the two or three greatest of all American poets."[7] Roger Lundin calls her "one of the major religious thinkers of her age," and says, "No other person in American history has become so famous in death after having been so anonymous in life."[8]

Dickinson's writing makes it clear that she had a sense of her worth, but even a supreme egotist could never have imagined the continuing influence or popularity of her work. Literary tastes ebb and flow, so there is no guarantee about the next generation or even the next decade, but one way or another, Emily Dickinson's poems seem certain to have a continuing audience.

## Emily Dickinson the Recluse

Dickinson gradually followed an increasingly private course. In her twentieth year she described the previous week as "a merry one in Amherst" and her town as "alive with fun this winter." In the years that followed, however, her associations outside her family and correspondence became very few. This wasn't surprising to her family. They were inclined to enjoy solitude. After Emily's death her sister Lavinia said Emily was withdrawn but that she "was always watching for the rewarding person to come." "She had to think," Lavinia said, "she was the only one of us who had that to do."[9]

Think she did. In 1862, she wrote 350 poems. About this time, she stopped visiting in the homes of her neighbors and discontinued going to church. In 1864 and 1865 she had to spend several months in Cambridge, Massachusetts, to receive eye treatments. After that she never again left Amherst. Beginning in the late 1860s, she never left the family's property, and from 1870 she dressed only in white. When people came to see her, she ordinarily talked to them only through a partially opened door.

With a few persons she remained the most cordial of communicators. She and Higginson maintained a lively correspondence, although he was troubled by her not being more involved in life. Elizabeth and Josiah Holland also were constant correspondents. Josiah, whose poem "There's a Song in the Air" is still widely sung at Christmas time, lifted Emily with the gracious quality of his faith. The God to whom Holland prayed, Emily said, "must be a friend."

Emily's most intense friendship, however, was with a widower, Otis Lord. He was eighteen years older than Emily. He became for a time the most important person in her life. Most of their correspondence was destroyed, at Emily's request, but what remains demonstrates the depth, passion, and intensity of their love for each other. It was the closest Emily came to marriage. Less than two years after they broke up, Otis died.

## Emily Dickinson and God

Then there was God. Several times in Emily's life–particularly in her friendship with Otis Lord and earlier with her sister-in-law, Susan Gilbert Dickinson–Emily spoke of persons as taking the place of God in her life. Emily was astute enough in her spiritual perception to verbalize what many of us might think but avoid bringing to expression. Pascal spoke of the God-shaped void that only God can fill. In truth, we humans try through all our days to expand persons, causes, affections, and a variety of less-worthy matters into the place only God can fill.

For Emily Dickinson, the God-shaped void was a lifelong issue. It had a context in her upbringing and in her knowledge of both the Bible and the hymns of the church. Roger Lundin says that in Emily's adulthood the only source she quoted more often than Shakespeare was the King James Bible. Nineteen Bibles form part of the Dickinson collection at Harvard University. They belonged to members of Emily's immediate family—and this in a day when you didn't have a plethora of translations to encourage multiple purchases.

But mostly Emily wrestled with God. She never found believing easy, not even as a young girl. Yet she found it even more difficult to pull away from God. At times she loved to be irreverent in her comments about both God and scripture, yet she never ceased to be drawn Godward:

> The abdication of Belief
> Makes the Behavior small—
> Better an ignis fatuus
> Than no illume at all.[10]

Her language is interesting. "Ignis fatuus," a *foolish light*, or *fool's light*, is better than no light at all. If this were the testimony of a simple soul in a revival service, one might smile at it. One ponders deeply at Emily Dickinson, however, wondering at the longing her words reveal.

Whatever her intermittent unhappiness with God, she makes no brief for an atheist. She relegates the atheist to an uncomplimentary company:

> How much the present moment means
> To those who've nothing more—
> The Fop—the Carp—the Atheist—[11]

Dickinson's gift for putting profound insights into a few words carries over to her handling of theology. How could one say more, and say it more poignantly, than this:

> How brittle are the Piers
> On which our Faith doth tread—
> No Bridge below doth totter so—

Yet none hath such a Crowd.
It is as old as God—
Indeed—'twas built by him—
He sent his Son to test the Plank,
And he pronounced it firm.[12]

Above all, Emily Dickinson clung to a belief in eternal life. So she wrote, in one of her longer poems,

Because I could not stop for Death—
He kindly stopped for me—
The Carriage held but just Ourselves—
And Immortality.[13]

But her most quoted lines on this subject are wonderfully simple, so much so that I remember reading them to my children from one of their collections of childhood poetry:

I never saw a Moor—
I never saw the Sea—
Yet know I how the Heather looks
And what a Billow be.
I never spoke with God
Nor visited in Heaven—
Yet certain am I of the spot
As if the Checks were given.[14]

## Emily Dickinson's Legacy

This is Emily Dickinson: premier poet, penetrating analyst of life and death, recluse in a white dress. And above all, as I see it, a person who walked again and again to the gates of God's Kingdom and stepped back, more pulled by her questions than by her certainties. Of course, only God can know where a human soul ultimately stands. But I am impressed that Emily's last written words, in a deathbed note to her cousins, announced that she was "called home." I think she knew her final address.

# CHAPTER 15

# Frances Willard

## The "Do-Everything" Woman

If you go to the Statuary Hall in the United States Capitol in Washington, D.C., you may be surprised to see who represents the State of Illinois. In truth, unless you've studied the history of social reform in America or know the unfolding story of women's rights and particularly women's suffrage, you may look at the statue and say, "Who's that?"

### Introducing Frances Willard

It's Frances Willard! No one in the late nineteenth century would have wondered who she was or why she was chosen to represent Illinois in the hall established by Congress to honor persons who had performed distinguished military or civic service or who were considered "worthy of this national commemoration." No one would have been surprised that she was the first woman to be so chosen.

### Basic Background

Frances Elizabeth Caroline Willard was born in Churchville, New York, in 1839. She graduated from North Western Female College in Evanston, Illinois, in 1859 and gave herself immediately to the field of education. In 1871 she was named president of the Evanston College for Ladies. Two years later, when the school merged with Northwestern University, Willard was named Dean of the Women's College at the University. The following year she became involved with the Woman's Christian Temperance Union, first as a lecturer, then as president of the Chicago and Illinois units. She became president of the national body in 1879, a position she held until her death in 1898. At the time, the WCTU was one of the most powerful organizations in America. Miss Willard founded a world temperance union in 1883.

She repeatedly expressed her desired to be ordained to the ministry, but her denomination, the Methodist Episcopal Church (one of the forebears of the United Methodist Church) refused at that time to ordain women. In 1889, she made a reasoned case for women's ordination in her book, *Woman in the Pulpit*. She was a prominent leader in reform politics in general, but particularly in the call for woman suffrage.

### Communities of Interest

Frances Willard appeals to anyone interested in the roots of the women's rights movement. Her personal record of leadership is almost without parallel, especially in its time. Her story also appeals to anyone with a passion for social reform. Her ability to combine such reform with an appreciation for conservative ideals is particularly impressive and instructive.

One might well tell the Frances Willard story on Mother's Day as an example of someone who never had biological children but who was mother to great numbers of people in her passion for justice and for the family. This can be an appropriate way of celebrating a popular holiday in a way that does not exclude those women who for one reason or another have never been mother to a physical family.

**SERMON** _____

# Frances Willard: *The "Do-Everything" Woman*

## Scripture Lesson: Proverbs 31:10–20, 30–31

Fame is not only fickle; it often has poor taste. We aren't sorry when the author of a superficial best seller is unknown a few years later. Only the most devoted students of politics can name the losing vice-presidential candidate from three elections ago. However, sometimes a new generation forgets figures of true prominence or lets them become a subject of only trivial reminiscence. Such an exit from national or world memory is particularly unfortunate when the person involved represented some grand or worthy cause.

## Frances Willard's Background

That's the case with Frances Willard. In the late nineteenth century she was popularly referred to as the "Saint Frances of American womanhood." On the day of her funeral, flags were lowered in Washington, D.C. and in Chicago, her headquarters city for many years. Her body was placed for viewing in Willard Hall at Chicago's Temple office building. Some thirty thousand people filed by in one day, most of them standing in February cold for an extended time before being able to enter the building. A biographer wrote, "[N]o woman before or since was so clearly on the day of her death this country's most honored woman."[1] From what I know of American history, I have to agree.

All this is in spite of the fact that she was never elected to a political office; indeed, she was never able to vote in a national election. Further, none of the causes to which she gave her powerful leadership succeeded within her lifetime, but many of those causes became an accepted part of American life. These include public kindergartens, separate correctional institutions for women, the vote for women, and Protestant ecumenism. She involved herself in virtually every major reform activity in the last quarter of the nineteenth century.

That's why I call her "The Do-Everything Woman." Although Frances Willard could concentrate on an issue with such intensity that it seemed almost to consume her, her vision was so broad she was always taking on new enthusiasms. Her last major public address, which Lady Henry Somerset had to read for her, was titled, "The Do Everything Policy." That phrase became the watchword for the organization she headed for so many years, the Woman's Christian Temperance Union. She was the vigorous personification of the term. It is impossible to tell the story of late nineteenth-century political and social history without referring again and again to Frances Willard.

There's some irony in what I've just said. Frances was born in September, 1839, in Churchville, New York, to Mary and Josiah Willard. When she was two years old, her father moved the family to Wisconsin, where he hoped to further his education. In time, he became a very successful farmer, a community leader, and a political leader. He was elected to the Wisconsin legislature as a member of the Free Soil party. When Abraham Lincoln visited the Wisconsin Agricultural Society in 1859, Josiah Willard introduced him.

However, he was hardly the person to father one of the two or three leading woman suffragists of the nineteenth century. He believed a woman's sphere of influence was the home. Although he accepted

Frances's becoming a teacher, he was never at peace with the idea of her earning her own living. He died in January, 1868, some years before Frances began to demonstrate her abilities as a leader. One wonders how he would have coped with the prominence that eventually marked her life, to say nothing of the role she played in the struggle for women's rights.

## Frances Willard's Religious Experience

Frances Willard had a mind of her own. For whatever role genetics plays in such matters, she could have inherited this quality from both her mother and her father. She showed it in breaking away from her father's philosophy about her place in society and in her ability all through her life to take a stand for unpopular causes.

The same independence showed itself in her religious experience. Although her family belonged to the Methodist church, at age twenty Frances still had not undergone a conversion experience—a religious coming-of-age emphasized in Methodism at the time. As a student at North Western Female College, a small Methodist school, she raised more than her share of questions. When the school had a religious revival, she at last agreed to go to the altar, out of her regard for the school's president. Later that evening, she wrote the president a long letter, confessing that she had been hypocritical in what she had done because she could not yet call herself a believer.

In June, 1859, ill with typhoid fever, Frances heard God speaking to her. She made a firm resolve to follow Jesus Christ. Some six months later, early in 1860, she joined the Methodist Church, where she remained for the rest of her life. She wrote in her diary, a few days after her affiliating with Methodism, "I honestly believe that I regard all churches, the branches rather of the one Church, with feelings of equal kindness and fellowship."[2] This was a remarkable statement for anyone to make at that time, particularly a woman of twenty. To come into the church with enthusiasm and commitment, yet to see farther than loyalty to a particular denomination was decidedly beyond the usual pattern. The Methodist church probably had no one more dedicated than Frances Willard. Certainly no Methodist layperson was more famous in her time. Still, she had room for all other Protestant bodies and eventually became very cordial with Roman Catholic leadership.

## Frances Willard Headed Nowhere

Bright and talented as Frances Willard was, her career path seemed headed in no particular direction. She held a variety of teaching posts, but with no evidence of progress. Nowadays we'd probably say that she was still trying to "find herself"—a phrase and concept that wouldn't have fit in Ms. Willard's time, even though it might have described her experience. One way or another, however, she did some "finding" through a time of expanding her world

Through the generosity of James Jackson, a man of considerable wealth, Frances and Jackson's daughter, Kate, traveled from the spring of 1868 through the fall of 1870, seeing much of Europe, Egypt, Turkey, and Palestine. In the process, Frances learned French and a bit of German and Italian. She also studied classical antiquity, art and architecture, and monarchial government. Frances had the capacity to make the most of this once-in-a-lifetime experience.

Particularly, she came away from her travels with a new perception of the role of women in the world. She observed at firsthand the abuses women were suffering in several parts of the world. She was convinced that she should give herself to the education of women. As she put it in a letter to a friend, she was going into an "earnest, ceaseless work for the baby daughters of a thousand homes who shall yet be happier and wiser because of my toil."

## Frances Willard the Educator

When the newly-formed Ladies College in Evanston, Illinois, looked for a president early in 1871, Frances Willard was the right person in the right place at the right time. The school was to be attached to Northwestern University but with freedom to function independently. The situation changed somewhat the following year. The school became the Women's College of Northwestern University, with Willard as dean, rather than president, in a structure that Willard herself had worked out.

Willard's career then came to a strange corner. Northwestern University got a new president, a rising young Methodist minister, Charles Fowler. He would eventually become editor of the denominational magazine the *Christian Advocate,* and then a Methodist bishop. Several years earlier, while Fowler was a seminary student, he and Frances became acquainted through Frances's brother Oliver. They fell in love and became engaged to marry. Some six months later, however, Frances broke the engagement. Her only explanation, expressed later in life, was that she wasn't prepared to abdicate her independence in the way marriage required. Considering the nature of her personality, her analysis may well have been correct.

Frances and Charles had remained good friends, but the new relationship—he as president of the University and she as Dean of its venturesome new women's school–simply proved unworkable. The facts seem to line up in Miss Willard's favor, but the power lay in Fowler's hands. Willard chose to resign. She referred later to this episode as the most painful experience of her life.

## Frances Willard and the Temperance Movement

Then a new door opened, one through which Frances would walk for the rest of her life. Alcohol consumption had become an increasingly serious problem in America. Women suffered particularly, because of alcohol's affect on family life. Thus, as reform movements sprang into action, women quickly were in the forefront. The issue came naturally to Frances. Her father had become involved in the temperance movement rather early as an honorary member of the Washingtonians. Frances had herself signed an abstinence pledge when she was not yet sixteen.

More important, from Frances's point of view, was the way the women's movement and the temperance movement coalesced in the winter of 1873–74. You could hardly imagine a more congenial marriage. At the time, temperance stood as the number one issue for women. To deal with the issue, women had to have political power. Such political power would come only through organizing. Different women had different views about where the organizing should lead. Some wanted full equality obtained via the ballot box. Others wanted only to become a moral influence. But one way or another, organizing was essential. Nothing made organizing more immediate and passionate than the power and prevalence of the liquor industry.

The temperance movement represented a dramatic change for Frances Willard. She moved from quiet Bible classes and evening devotions with the young women at the college, to a life that combined preaching, praying with derelicts, and raising money in temperance rallies in the churches of Greater Chicago.

## Frances Willard the Preacher

She soon discovered that preaching came naturally to her. No doubt she was now benefiting from her childhood years of disciplined writing and from her long years of fascination with words. She also possessed an innate ability to "do business" with an audience. People responded to her fervor, her vigor, and her compelling sincerity as much as to her well-crafted words. This gift accelerated her rise in the temperance movement.

At an organizing national convention in November, 1874, she was easily elected corresponding secretary on the first ballot, even though she was a relative newcomer to the movement. Speaking fees also began to augment her modest income. In early 1877, she joined the staff of Dwight L. Moody for a short time. Moody was at that time the best known evangelist in both the United States and Great Britain. Even though the relationship was brief, it added to Willard's experience and popularity.

Women's work and temperance remained Willard's special passion. She gave herself to them with tremendous energy. Over a period of several years, she visited more than one thousand American towns and cities. This often meant inconvenient and tiring travel. She managed slowly to bring together the advocates of suffrage and temperance. Often they were the same persons, but just as often they were isolated from one another. Some of the temperance workers, for instance, found the suffrage movement too radical for their tastes. Some of the suffrage people weren't at home in the evangelical atmosphere that dominated the temperance movement.

Frances Willard could move easily in both circles. On the one hand, she was a consummate political animal. I suspect if she had been born a century later, she might well have been America's first woman president. On the other hand, she was unabashedly devout. She saw her work with women as a divine calling. She wrote that once when she was on her knees alone "there was borne in upon my mind, as I believe, from loftier regions, the declaration, 'You are to speak for woman's ballot as a protection to her home and tempted loved ones from the tyranny of drink.'"[3] Whatever one may think of such a sense of divine leading, you can hardly doubt the force it would give to a person's work and influence.

## Frances Willard, the Temperance Union President

In 1879, at the age of 40, she was elected president of the national Woman's Christian Temperance Union. She led it to become the largest women's organization in the United States. If she had chosen a pattern she wished to emulate, it could well have been King Lemuel's words in Proverbs 31:

She girds herself with strength,
    and makes her arms strong...
She opens her hand to the poor,
    and reaches out her hands to the needy. (Prov. 31:17, 20)

She had charm to spare and some judged her physically attractive, but she would have preferred the biblical description:

Charm is deceitful, and beauty is vain,
  but a woman who fears the LORD is to be praised
    (Prov. 31:30).

The writer of Proverbs concluded that for such a woman, "let her works praise her in the city gates" (Prov. 31:31). Frances received just such praise in wondrous abundance: in cities, small towns, and villages in every part of the country. When she addressed the WCTU convention in New York City in 1888 in the new Metropolitan Opera House, four thousand people joined the four hundred delegates to hear her. Hundreds more were turned away.

## Frances Willard, the "Do-Everything" Woman

She became the "do-everything" woman, pleading for a grocer's list of causes in which she believed. Temperance and suffrage led the way, but she affiliated herself with an impressive variety of commitments. "Virtues," she said, "like hounds, hunt in packs." She feared that "a one-sided movement makes for one-sided advocates."[4]

She carried her fervor to England joining forces with Lady Henry Somerset. She spent most of the period from 1892 to 1896 in England, where she enjoyed great popularity. Gradually her health broke. Try as she would, she could not complete some of the fund-raising to which she had committed herself. On February 17, 1898, she died, shortly after saying, "How beautiful to be with God."

## Frances Willard's Legacy

The abolition of poverty, toward which she had aimed with her involvement in Christian socialism, had not been accomplished. Woman suffrage would come nearly a generation later. So too would the prohibition amendment, which would be repudiated within a generation after its establishment. Her strong appeal for the ordination of women in her book *Woman in the Pulpit* (1888) would have to wait roughly half a century before it would succeed in her own denomination. The woman some would describe as the greatest woman orator in America and perhaps America's best-known woman for nearly two decades saw her "do everything" campaign never quite make it. But she was a happy warrior. I'm almost certain she would have said it was worth the fight. Without a doubt, she would have been ready to do it again.

# CHAPTER 16

# Charles M. Sheldon
## *The Preacher as Novelist*

Some years ago, well into a sixteen-year pastorate, I was searching for a way to begin a new calendar year with strength. People are ready to be challenged when a new year opens. I was hoping for a challenge with more sustained impact than a single sermon might give. I experienced a moment of inspiration that I feel was a gift from God. I preached from Charles M. Sheldon's late nineteenth-century novel, *In His Steps.*

This became a five-week series, beginning with the basic story, then successive sermons on "What Would Jesus Do? With Religion, with Business, with Community Life, with Wealth." The response was as good as a parish pastor could hope for—perhaps partly because the sermons "tangibilitated": they spoke to people in the continuing questions of their daily lives, and they called them to rise higher.

## Introducing Charles Sheldon

*Basic Information*

Charles M. Sheldon was born in 1857 in Wellsville, New York. Educated at Phillips Academy, Brown University, and Andover Theological Seminary, he prepared for a life in congregational ministry, following in the steps of his father before him. In 1899 he began what proved to be a lifelong call to the Central Congregational Church in Topeka, Kansas. He also had a relationship of some twenty-six years with the *Christian Herald,* perhaps the most influential

Protestant publication at the time in America. He was a moderate theological liberal with a passion for social reform. He died in 1946.

### Communities of Interest

Charles Sheldon appeals to people across a wide spectrum, as wide, I might say, as the varieties of people you saw wearing WWJD symbols a few years ago. The socially conscious are inspired by his full-scale and early support for the rights of women, of African Americans, and of minorities in general; and by his untiring efforts for world peace and abolition of poverty. The evangelical resonate with his commitment to live by the question, "What would Jesus do?" His story could well be told on a Sunday celebrating race relations or peace and justice, including perhaps Labor Day Sunday.

## SERMON _____

# Charles M. Sheldon: *The Preacher as Novelist*

## Scripture Lesson: Mark 8:34–38

People used to speak of writing "the great American novel." I think we've given up on that idea, perhaps because no one knows how to define "great." Is it the novel with the biggest sales? If so, some of the most poorly written works might be most likely to win the prize. Is it a novel that appeals to the literary community? I suspect it would be nearly impossible for that rather indefinite group to reach any measure of agreement.

If we were to say that a great novel is one that has influenced large numbers of persons over an extended period of time, I would like to make a case for a novel that was written in 1896. This novel remains in print today in a rather wide variety of editions. Not long ago, the key phrase from this novel became an acronym seen almost everywhere–among young and old, poor and middle class, educated and barely literate: WWJD–"What would Jesus do?" The novel's author was a preacher, and this novel *In His Step,* was without a doubt his best known sermon, or more correctly, series of sermons.

### Charles M. Sheldon's Background

The preacher/author was Charles M. Sheldon. Let me say, before I go further, that I know Sheldon's *In His Steps* is not great literature. It is an easy read, with a simple plot, generally uncomplicated characters, and sometimes wooden dialogue. Sheldon himself would agree that his novel lacked greatness. He was enough of a student of literature to know the difference.

One Saturday afternoon when Sheldon was in his mid-teens and a student at Phillips Academy, he came upon a secondhand copy of *Les Miserables.* It cost a dollar, and he had only $1.17 in his pocket. The train back to Andover would cost 63 cents. Sheldon paid for the book and walked the 21 miles along the railroad track back to Andover. Arriving at 2 a.m., he threw a log on the fire in his student room and read until he had finished Book One. Then, while others in the dormitory were getting up, he went to bed, satisfied! I submit that someone with such tastes would know a good novel when he saw one—or when he wrote one.

## Writing/Preaching the Novel

As I said a moment ago, Sheldon's novel was in truth a series of sermons. The church in Topeka, Kansas, of which he was the pastor, had a Sunday evening service. To build up attendance at that service, he began writing novels that he would read as his sermon. He mastered the skill of writing in such a way that he would leave the audience hanging in suspense at the end of each chapter. That meant they would return (in fact, could hardly wait to return) the following Sunday evening.

Incidentally, he stood in a rather noble literary tradition in this kind of serial writing. Charles Dickens, George Eliot, Thackeray, Trollope, and a host of lesser persons produced some of their finest work in this fashion, not as sermons, but as weekly installments in newspapers or magazines.

*In His Steps* was the seventh such series Charles Sheldon offered his people. He began reading it on Sunday evening, October 4, 1896, and it became an immediate success with his people. An independent religious magazine, *The Advance,* paid $75.00 for serial rights for publication, releasing it chapter by chapter. They then published the complete book in June, 1897. The cloth edition sold for one dollar, and the paperback, for twenty-five cents. Hundreds of thousands were sold.

Before long, literally dozens of publishers began printing the book. The Woolworth stores brought it out in a dime edition. Any number of newspapers and magazines also released it in serial form. More than 25 British and European publishers brought out their own editions. A grocer in Scotland commissioned his own copy for distribution to his customers, with the name of his store printed at the bottom of each page.

## The Novel, a Simple Story

*In His Steps* is a simple story, but an enormously appealing one. It begins with a touch of melodrama. A young man stops at the home of the Reverend Henry Maxwell one Friday morning, seeking help in finding work. The pastor is kind, but hurried; he can't do much to help the man. That Sunday the service at Maxwell's church focused on a theme much like our scripture lesson of the day. In that text, Jesus sensed that he would soon be arrested and brought to trial. He threw out a challenge to his disciples and to those who contemplated being disciples. "If any want to become my followers, let them deny themselves and take up their cross and follow me" (Mk. 8:34). With all of our talk about Christianity, the issue finally comes to this: will we follow Jesus Christ; will we take up a cross at his call?

Such was the mood in the service that morning at the mythical Central Church. The choir sang an arrangement of the hymn, "Jesus, I my cross have taken, / all to leave and follow Thee," after which the church's soprano soloist had sung, "Where He leads me, I will follow."

The sermon was strong and polished. When the pastor finished, the young man who had solicited help two days before came to the front of the church. "I'm not drunk and I'm not crazy," he explained, before going on to tell his sad story. A printer, he had lost his job ten months before, replaced by the invention of the linotype machine. Since his wife's death, he had been tramping over the country, seeking work, without success. "It seems to me," he said, "there's an awful lot of trouble in the world that somehow wouldn't exist if all the people who sing such songs went and lived them out. I suppose I don't understand. But what would Jesus do?" A few seconds later, he slumped to the floor. A few days later, he died.

From this setting, the Reverend Mr. Maxwell felt challenged to call his congregation to deal with the man's question: "What would Jesus do?" The following Sunday, he pleaded with his people to accept the challenge to use this question as a guide in all their daily conduct. The novel is realistic. About fifty persons accept the call, but the vast majority of the people do not. I suspect this is about the way it would be in any good, average congregation. As time goes by, the church threatens to split. The novel follows several of the key persons who take the pledge. It faces honestly some of the issues that ensue when people seek discipleship with real integrity.

## The Novel's Context

The novel reflects some of the optimism of the 1890s, a period when many in American religious life felt the kingdom of God was very near. They anticipated that the twentieth century might well prove to be "the Christian century," a time when peace, prosperity, equality of opportunity, and justice would sweep over the land–and from America, over the rest of the world. Sheldon's book fed on that optimism while acknowledging that its goal would not be easily attained.

Sheldon soon had firsthand opportunity to see how difficult it is to live out the gospel in our real world. I mentioned earlier how enormously popular Sheldon's novel became. It seemed that everywhere you turned the book was being printed and marketed. Here's the dark underside. When the original edition of the book was released, the publisher failed in a minor detail to obtain a valid copyright. As a result, the book was fair game to any publisher without paying royalties. This expedited publication of the book by those who wanted to make a quick dollar or by those who simply wanted to see the book more widely distributed, but it brought no reward to Sheldon or to the original publisher.

Of course, it could hardly be more ironic that this book should be exploited in a way diametrically at odds with the message of the book. Legal, yes, but ethical, no. All of which goes to show that if you want to live in our world by the rule, "What would Jesus do?" you must be ready to suffer disappointment in the way people respond to your intentions.

## Living in His Steps

No doubt many would say that Charles M. Sheldon was naïve and unrealistic, but no one could seriously doubt the toughness of his commitment. *In His Steps* was not simply a story to him; he tried to live it out. One of his first pastoral projects in Topeka was to work for the betterment of a black settlement known as Tennesseetown. He lived there for three weeks, in the midst of unmitigated poverty, so he could grasp the situation firsthand. He went on to establish the first black kindergarten west of the Mississippi.

Since one of the main characters in Sheldon's book was a newspaper publisher, in 1900 the publishers of the *Topeka Daily Capitol* invited Sheldon to run the newspaper by his Christian convictions for one week. It was quite a revolution! The masthead listed every employee, including janitor and galley boy. Bylines were required on all stories to keep reporters responsible. Writers had to avoid slang. After interviews, reporters were to show the resulting article to the subject for approval. Crime news was to be limited, with commentary on how the crime might have been prevented. Employees were asked not to drink, swear, or smoke at work. The society editor got an assignment to cover an average day in Topeka, writing about the time and money wasted in social frivolity on that particular day. This included an itemized statement of the cost of the day—a job the society editor reveled in! The next day the newspaper ran an editorial suggesting that the money might better have been sent to relieve the famine that was at that time devastating India.

One thing more. During the week Sheldon edited the *Topeka Daily Capitol,* he not only accepted no advertising that he felt was "suggestive and coarse," but he also refused ads from Kansas City merchants. He reasoned that they were competing with the merchants in Topeka. He reasoned that "a home paper should protect home merchants." One wonders how Sheldon would respond to the dot.com businesses in our day.

## Ahead of or behind the Times?

I hesitate to use the terms "ahead of his times" or "behind the times" for anyone, because I'm not sure anyone knows enough about the times to judge what is "ahead" and what is "behind." When I tell you where Charles Sheldon stood in a variety of matters, I'm quite sure you'll not know where to put him.

He served briefly as Topeka's police commissioner. He called for a Christian police force with police acting as missionaries. Our generation would be uneasy with that idea. As police commissioner, Sheldon appointed the first two policewomen. This was roughly one hundred years ago. See how recently your city began having women officers, and you will see him as a progressive. He supported the idea of Sunday observance, which would please contemporary conservatives, but he argued against large personal fortunes, which might offend those same conservatives.

He considered speculators "leeches on society," because they actually produced nothing. When we consider some of the financial scandals of the past few years, we might think that we should listen carefully to Sheldon's ideas . He worked earnestly for the prohibition amendment, which discredits him with a generation that has always been told that this amendment was a failure. He promised that if he ever succeeded in closing the saloons, he would then go to work on the problem of overeating. He sounds like the most prescient of twenty-first century social observers.

## Charles M. Sheldon's Legacy

Perhaps the best thing that can be said for Charles M. Sheldon is that he never stopped trying to do what he recommended in his most popular novel. Like a sizeable percentage of middle-class families of the time, the Sheldons had servants. Dr. Sheldon wanted them to eat with the family, but Mrs. Sheldon could never accept this idea. She was careful not to overpay the help, but he would slip them extra money on the side. As a matter of fact, he gave away his money so freely to anyone who seemed in need that Mrs. Sheldon put him on a five-dollar allowance to be sure he didn't simply give away all they had. He was, in truth, world famous, but he seemed never to know it. Unlike many people with such recognition, he continued to make himself accessible to any who called on him.

Our text of the day says that those who would follow Jesus should "take up their cross." That's a demanding word, and one not too often heard in our preaching. That's too bad, because our generation needs desperately to see such Christian heroism. Not only does our generation need to see self-sacrifice and heroism, but also those of us who follow Christ need to discover that while the demand is tough, the way of life is very wonderful. Sheldon put it simply: "Begin the day with a song and end it with a prayer." It sounds as if Sheldon had discovered another fact about following Christ: as Jesus put it, "For my yoke is easy, and my burden is light" (Mt. 11:30).

When I look at Sheldon's theology and economics, I find that I am sometimes to his right and sometimes to his left. But when I look at the man, I think he's just about where I would like to be. I marvel that it was a preacher who wrote a best-selling novel that still finds a market today—and that the novel was a series of sermons! I don't claim that it is the great American novel, but I doubt that many—if any—have had such continuing influence for human good.

# CHAPTER 17

# George Washington Carver
## *He Saw God's Wonder in a Peanut*

I was excited several years ago to be on the campus of Simpson College in Indianola, Iowa, because it meant a chance to see the school where George Washington Carver began his college education. My pleasure was still greater when one of my seminars took me to a science building named for Dr. Carver. I had known Dr. Carver's name for most of my rather long life, so it was a kind of pilgrimage to visit the campus that first accepted this irregular student and started him on his way to international achievement and recognition.

### Introducing George Washington Carver

The Carver story needs to be told. His name was an icon in my grade school days. Those were less complicated days and a time–I speak with prejudice–when we were trained to look for heroes with demonstrated substance. Dr. Carver's story is a lesson in race relations, a study in perseverance and the ability to overcome obstacles, and an immersion in a personality marked by indomitable graciousness and good will. The person who doesn't learn something from the story of George Washington Carver is either a finished saint or a fool.

### Basic Background

George Washington Carver was born a slave, in 1859, by best estimate, near Diamond Grove, Missouri. Night raiders stole him and his slave mother when he was a baby. His owner, Moses Carver, was never able to retrieve George's mother, but is said to have bought back the baby for a racehorse. From his earliest days the boy was fascinated by plants and rocks. He demonstrated uncanny insight into plant life.

His education was a piecemeal affair until Simpson College. He went from there to Iowa State College, from which he graduated in 1894. He stayed on as an assistant botanist until 1896, when he joined the work of Booker T. Washington at Tuskegee (Alabama) Institute. He remained there until his death in 1943. He developed more than 300 products from peanuts and 118 products from the sweet potato. In the process, he brought a whole new system of agriculture to a section of America that had relied almost entirely on a diminishing cotton economy.

### Communities of Interest

Dr. Carver's story has unique significance to the African American population, to children and young people of any race, and to persons who have been forced to work with serious limitations. One can tell his story effectively on Martin Luther King Day, Independence Day Sunday, or Labor Day Sunday. Sometimes the most effective approach to race relations comes when the subject is approached obliquely, for example, by using the Carver story as an instance of Christian vocation for the Sunday near Labor Day.

**SERMON** _____

# George Washington Carver:
## *He Saw God's Wonder in a Peanut*

### Scripture Lesson: Genesis 1:26–31
(Dr. Carver looked upon verse 29 as a key to his work.)

No one can predict where God will plant another genius. We expect a prophet Isaiah, with his background in a royal court, but not an Amos, coming from tending sheep. We understand how God can use the apostle Paul, who was trained by one of the finer scholars of the first century world, but how does God make something of a fisherman like Peter?

And where does God find the pattern for a George Washington Carver?

## George Washington Carver's Background

Carver's story has been neglected in recent years, and that's a pity. If we marvel at all these days, it is at the apparently unlimited possibilities of plastics or the expanding mysteries of the computer. Once upon a time, however, a remarkable man worked alone in the simplest kind of laboratory without any trained assistance until the latter years of his life. In so doing he found endless marvels in the plants of the field. Eventually, his work won international acclaim, yet he often had to enter the back door of the hotels in which he was the featured banquet speaker.

George Washington Carver was born a slave near Diamond Grove, Missouri, in 1859. The date is approximate; careful records were not kept for slave births. While he was still an infant, night raiders stole him and his mother, Mary. Moses Carver, the slaves' owner, hired a man to hunt down the thieves and bring back Mary and her baby. He succeeded only in bringing back the sickly infant. Moses Carver gave the man a racehorse as his reward.

The Carvers had professed not to believe in slavery and had purchased Mary only as a way of having help in their house and farm. They demonstrated their beliefs in the way they nursed George through a number of illnesses. Since George wasn't strong enough for farm work, Mrs. Carver trained him in the kitchen, giving him skills that helped him survive in some of his most difficult years. Meanwhile, the boy studied plants and rocks. They fascinated him. He seemed to commune with them. In turn, they told him their secrets. At least it appeared that way to those who sought the boy's advice with plants that died for others and grew for him.

## George Washington Carver on the Move

When he was ten, George left the Carver home and walked to Neosho, Missouri. By what some would call luck and others would call providence, he stumbled upon an African American family who made him their own. Now he was able to go to school. His teacher was a member of his own race, but George disliked him because the teacher was "ashamed of being a Negro."[1] George not only maintained a lifelong pride in his race, but he also dedicated himself to instilling that pride in others.

George then began a series of moves. I consider myself part of a hardy generation, but I marvel at a boy of thirteen who moves to Kansas with virtually no possessions, with no connections, and with a skin color  that invited anything from exploitation to rejection to crowd violence. Yes, at thirteen, George Washington Carver began moving from place to place. When he was mistreated, he managed to take it in stride. He seemed to possess unlimited good will and a dignity that was never diminished no matter what others said or did. When I think of his genius, I think of course of the virtual miracles he worked with plants, but his genius for quiet self-respect is almost as great as his scientific genius and harder to analyze or emulate.

## George Washington Carver the College Student

That genius received its greatest test when he appeared at the college that had accepted his application but immediately rejected him when they discovered his color. For someone with such a passion for knowledge, this injustice was devastating.

That summer, however, he learned about and was accepted at Simpson College, a small Methodist liberal arts school in Indianola, Iowa. By this time he was in his late twenties. Fifty years later, the president of Simpson College visited Dr. Carver in his famous laboratory, and Carver explained that all his work had resulted from the vision he had received at Simpson. When the president asked him to explain, Carver said simply, "It was at Simpson I realized that I was a human being."[2]

Some years earlier, in the Presbyterian Church in Olathe, Kansas, George had accepted Christ as his "personal Redeemer." I suspect that the acceptance at Simpson College was nothing less than a continuation of this redemption. George Washington Carver was on his way.

## George Washington Carver the Botanist

He went from Simpson College to Iowa State College at Ames, where he received a Master of Science degree in 1894. He remained at the school as an assistant botanist, beginning a fungus collection that eventually grew to some 20,000 species. Carver's career at Ames had unlimited promise. He was a favorite with students and colleagues, and the school was known as one of the finest agricultural schools in America. Then in 1896, Booker T. Washington invited him to join the faculty of the Tuskegee Institute in Alabama, a school Washington had founded fifteen years before to train African Americans to become teachers, masons, tradesmen, and skilled laborers.

Carver immediately saw this call as the purpose of his life. We can sense the piety that was at work in Carver in the conclusion of his letter of acceptance. He wrote to Washington, "May the Lord pour out his choicest blessing upon you and your work. Yours for

Christ, Geo. W. Carver." In a letter a week later, Carver promised his cooperation with Washington to do "all I can *through Christ who strengtheneth me* to better the condition of our people."[3]

## George Washington Carver at Tuskegee

Life at Tuskegee did not prove easy. Booker and George were both strong personalities, who had come to their places of responsibility by great inner toughness. Carver was a gentle man but a very determined one. His greatest joy, and certainly his most effective arena of achievement, was in the solitude of a laboratory. Washington was an aggressive administrator. He knew where he wanted the Tuskegee Institute to go, and he was confident of his own judgment in getting it there.

At times the two men clashed; once Carver tendered his resignation. He had come to Tuskegee for one thousand dollars a year and never allowed his salary to be increased, but he had a sense of personal dignity, and he knew where his talents should be employed.

On the other hand, Carver gave himself unreservedly to every imaginable request. Let a woman who loved roses and who wondered why her plant was dying, come to the professor, and he would solve her problem, no matter how many visits or letters might be needed. Any poor sharecropper could get his counsel without charge. The person who felt so benefited by Carver's knowledge that he sent fifty or one hundred dollars in appreciation would find the money returned in the next mail. Carver felt that his knowledge was a gift from the Creator, and therefore he must make it a gift to anyone who needed it. He also knew who he was and where he should invest his energy. He could and would defend that conviction as stubbornly as he could pursue an elusive scientific question.

## George Washington Carver and the Peanut

His particular passion was for the poor southern farmer, white or black. Cotton had been their one-crop economy. When the crop failed, the soil became depleted, or the market weakened, disaster loomed. Carver set out to diversify: first with the sweet potato, then with the soybean and pecan, and most famously, with the peanut. The peanut had more protein pound for pound than did sirloin, more carbohydrates than did potatoes. On one occasion, Dr. Carver worked with a class of senior girls at the Institute in preparing a five-course meal for Mr. Washington and nine guests: soup, mock chicken, salad, bread, candy, cookies, ice cream, coffee. All were made from peanuts.

In his earlier years, Carver had learned the difference "between good, rich, Jersey milk and just plain boardinghouse milk." So when he began making milk from the peanut, he addressed God as he often did: "Mr. Creator, shall I make rich, Jersey milk with cream or just plain boardinghouse milk?" He felt that God's answer was for Jersey richness.[4]

But nutrition was not the only goal of his experiments. Peanuts were also good for soap and ink, and the 118 products from sweet potatoes included flour, shoe blacking, and candy. When the Institute built its new Dorothy Hall, Carver noted that the walls were kalsomined, the woodwork stained, and the windows painted, all with native clay from the region. Later that year when the school asked for one hundred gallons of pink, gray, yellow, and buff kalsomine to brighten up their buildings, Dr. Carver explained that all the colors had come from a ditch near Tompkins Hall. His eye discovered wonders everywhere, wonders simply waiting to be discovered. He followed a simple formula, as he explained once to a meeting of the Woman's Board of Domestic Missions of the Reformed Church: "Anything will give up its secrets, if you love it enough."

As the wider world came to know of the genius at Tuskegee, he became a traveler. He spoke on college campuses, to church groups, and to every imaginable agricultural and scientific body. One of his greatest triumphs came in 1921. The Ways and Means Committee of the United States Senate invited him to appear before it on behalf of a tariff to protect the peanut farmer. As he approached the podium, one Senator asked, "I suppose if you have plenty of peanuts and watermelons, you're perfectly happy?"[5] Dr. Carver was used to people whose sense of humor was insensitive to others, so he took the jibe in stride. He was assigned ten minutes to tell his story, but after an hour and forty-five minutes the committee gave him a standing ovation.

## George Washington Carver's Values

Two other notable personalities from Carver's era sought to enlist his genius. Thomas A. Edison sent his chief engineer, Miller Hutcheson, to talk with Carver. On the basis of that conversation, Edison offered Dr. Carver a salary in six figures to join his laboratory staff. Carver's answer was simple: he had enough already. If one thousand dollars a year was enough, of what value would there be in multiplying it by one hundred or more?[6]

Carver found an immediate bond with Henry Ford. On one occasion the two men participated in a joint interview. A reporter asked Mr. Ford to answer the next question. The industrialist answered, "No. Just ask Dr. Carver. He knows about me. I agree with everything he thinks, and he thinks the same way I do."[7] Ford built a school and named it for Carver along with a guest cabin memorial at Greenfield Village. Perhaps his greatest tribute of friendship, however, was his gift to Dr. Carver of a cup and saucer his mother had brought to the United States as a bride.

As a prophet, Dr. Carver eventually found acceptance in his home country, but his first major honor came from Great Britain. In 1916 the prestigious Royal Society for the Encouragement of Arts, Manufactures, and Commerce elected him a fellow. The first school to award him an honorary doctorate was his alma mater, Simpson College, in 1928. The honors rolled in, although not without pain. When he arrived at the Hotel New Yorker in New York City to give an address, the hotel refused to recognize his reservation. He sat quietly in the lobby for six hours while his publisher threatened to sue the hotel and the New York *Post* demanded that something be done. At last it was.

## George Washington Carver's Faith

As surely as one cannot understand the musical genius of Johann Sebastian Bach without exploring his Christian faith, so we have to know George Washington Carver as a Christian before we can know him as a scientist. He would have been the first to insist on this basic fact. He testified to it often and eloquently. He called his laboratory, "God's Little Workshop." He said that he "leaned upon" Genesis 1:29: "And God said, Behold, I have given you every herb bearing seed, which is upon the face of all the earth, and every tree, in the which is the fruit of a tree yielding seed; to you it shall be for meat" (KJV). On February 12, 1934, Carver told his friends at Tuskegee how he went about his work. "First, I go into the woods and gather specimens, and listen to what God has to say to me. After I have had my morning talk with God, I go to my laboratory and begin to carry out His wishes for the day, and if I fail it's my failure, and if I succeed then God's will has been done."[8]

The great saints have always been marked by a friendship with God that is startling in both its intimacy and its reverence. Dr. Robert Bell, who was close to Carver in the last years of his life, met with him often for prayer. "When I visited him in his laboratory," Bell said, "he would often bow his head, sitting at the desk, and speak to God as to a person present in the room."

That's also the way he died. At about four o'clock in the afternoon, Dr. Carver asked James Lomax, the personal aide who had been with him for four years, what he was doing. "Preparing your meal," the young man said. Carver replied, "Yes, they are also preparing for me in the other world." Those were his final words.[9]

CHAPTER 18

# It Was a Very Good Year
### Frank Laubach and
### E. Stanley Jones

Sometimes we preachers search desperately for gold and find none, while other times we stumble upon a cache in spite of ourselves. The sermon you're about to read came in the latter category. As I was on the verge of 1984, I happened upon the fact that two Christian statesmen, E. Stanley Jones and Frank Laubach, were born in 1884. Of course, I was sensitive to the fact that 1984, the year we were then about to enter, was ominous to the ear and eye because of George Orwell's novel. The result can be found in this sermon.

I suspect that every year has some potential for a sermon on this model. You need not wait for two great personalities to produce an anniversary time; you might even discover some dramatic merit in working with a noble figure and an ignoble one. After all, *Time* magazine uses both for its cover stories, since both make history. Or you might use a well-known personality and a relatively obscure one, thereby raising the question as to who deserves a larger place in history.

Nor is it necessary to work only with birth centennials or bi-centennials. One can also use the date of death, or the date of a person's watershed action. Martin Luther is more easily remembered for the Wittenberg Door and 1517 than for his birth date of 1483. Nor is there anything wrong with a fifty-year marker, or a sesquicentennial.

It is important, however, to learn as much as you can about the era and the particular year, so the date means more than four simple

149

digits. You'll find several books that can help with this kind of information. *The Bicentennial Almanac,* edited by Calvin D. Linton and issued in 1976, is full of data about each year from 1776 to 1975. Each volume of *Twenty Centuries of Great Preaching* contains a foldout chart indicating items of political, cultural, and intellectual history overlapping the time lines of specific preachers. A good research librarian can lead you to other helpful volumes.

Ours is not a historically astute age, but we still have the capacity for historical curiosity. Even those who are most severely captive to the contemporary, can find themselves enchanted when pages of the past begin to come alive.

## SERMON _____

# Frank Laubach and E. Stanley Jones:
## It Was a Very Good Year

### Scripture Lesson: Psalm 126

Our American ancestors had good reason to be apprehensive as they entered the New Year a century ago. Perhaps "1884" didn't sound as ominous as did "1984," since their generation didn't have the benefit of George Orwell's novel and the peculiar significance of 1984. But in 1884, they had troubles enough and reasons enough for feeling uneasy. America was stumbling through an economic recession while still trying to find its way out of the continuing aftermath of the Civil War. The assassination of President James Garfield had stunned the nation.

So from all appearances 1884 would be a difficult year. It was an election year! James Blaine was running against Grover Cleveland. Historians say they waged one of the dirtiest political campaigns in our nation's history. Ferment rocked the land. Early in the year, Susan B. Anthony led one hundred demonstrators to the White House to urge the president to support woman suffrage. Persons captivated by disaster headlines had more than their fill in 1884. A steamer wreck off the coast of Massachusetts cost 103 lives. A coal mine disaster in Virginia claimed 112 lives. The "Great Flood of 1884" devastated Lawrenceburg, Indiana. When a rescue party found the Greely Arctic Expedition, only seven of the twenty-six men remained alive.

No doubt the doomsayers had a good inventory of darkness in 1884. Some must have said, "Times have never been worse," only to be answered, "Well, it may not be hopeless, but I venture it's pretty nearly so." If someone asked, "Do you think this old world will ever make it to the year 1900?" a friend was likely to answer (perhaps while pondering Europe's turmoil), "I seriously doubt it."

As it turned out, 1884 proved to be a very good year: the cornerstone of the Statue of Liberty was laid in August of 1884, establishing a setting toward which peoples in nearly every part of the world have looked for hope. Only careful students of history recall the rancor of the 1884 political campaign, shameful as it was, but the Statue of Liberty continues to send out its beam of inspiration.

In addition to the Statue of Liberty, other lights began shining in 1884. I doubt that anyone could have guessed what wonderful things were happening. Even those with the most perceptive view of the future, rarely see the most important promises. Our problem is that we inevitably look for our prospects in the wrong places. Plus, we do so with such short-term vision. We're not to be blamed for this. We're following a reasonable pattern, and we're looking where you'd expect to look, in likely and predictable places. But we simply can't expect life's greatest events to isolate themselves in likely and predictable places.

In 1884, people looked to Washington, D.C., to New York City, and to Boston. I can't blame them; after all, that's where the media have trained us to expect our answers. If the prospects aren't in government, business, or education, where would they be?

I'm sure no one, or almost no one, looked for anything important to happen that year in Benton, Pennsylvania, or Clarksville, Maryland. I venture that even the proudest citizens of those towns didn't expect much of importance to happen where they lived. But it did.

## Frank Laubach's Background

Let's take Benton, Pennsylvania, where, in 1884, Frank Laubach was born. In 1915, at thirty-one years of age, he completed his Doctor of Philosophy degree at Columbia University. He headed to the Island of Mindanao in the southern Philippines to be a missionary. If being born in Benton, Pennsylvania, didn't guarantee eventual obscurity, Laubach had found an even more certain path to obscurity—being a missionary on an island in the Philippines.

It's strange how we underestimate missionaries and their influence. After all, they have to be a special breed to have a vision for a world so far from their own and, in many instances, so different. A missionary's world is never limited to Ohio or Iowa or Pennsylvania, or even to the United States. Somehow they have eyes and heart to see faraway places and obscure ones. Nor is their vision limited to the more obvious prospects, either in places or in persons. Almost by definition, a missionary sees potential where others see nothing. If a typical missionary were to turn this adventuresome talent into the world of business, he or she might easily become a successful, financial entrepreneur.

## Frank Laubach's Vision

Frank Laubach got a vision. I don't know if it was a mystical vision, though he was later known as one of the world's great Christian mystics. I only know that he became burdened for the masses of people on our earth who are illiterate. He came to call these folks "The Silent Billion," though their number was actually much larger. He believed that these masses of people would always be exploited politically and financially, and that they would never be able to enjoy the divine potential of their lives until they could learn to read and to write.

In a sense, this was an unlikely turn of mind for a Columbia University Ph.D. We expect such a person to become involved in more erudite pursuits, teaching rather sophisticated material to other scholars or potential scholars. Instead, Frank Laubach found himself squatting on the ground next to scantily-dressed, illiterate humans, trying to find the quickest way to teach them to read. He had only one guiding principle: "Nobody knows whether a lesson is right but the illiterate. If it works, it is right."[1] Come to think of it, I wish some of my professors had lived by such a rule, and I wonder if I live it when I'm in the teaching role. The most successful business people insist that the customer is always right. Probably the best teachers follow the same rule.

## Frank Laubach's Payoff

Eventually Laubach's natural genius, his well-trained mind, and his willingness to learn from others began to pay off. He developed a method called "each one teach one," a volunteer method of promoting literacy. His picture-word syllable literacy charts were effective with even the most primitive peoples. He worked with the rule that anyone he taught to read must agree to teach another person. Reading is not something to be hoarded, but to be shared.

I don't know how to estimate how far Dr. Laubach's programs now reach. Within a bare thirty years, he became coauthor of more than 200 primers in over 165 languages. By that time, at least sixty million people had become readers through his method. Nowadays, hundreds of American communities employ the same type of program to teach the hidden illiterates of our cities and rural areas. Norman Cousins, past editor of *Saturday Review* and someone who knew about literacy at quite another level, called Laubach "one of the noblest human beings of our time."

But Laubach wasn't content simply to teach persons to read. Noble as it was to help persons get hold of their intellectual potential, Laubach also wanted them to grasp their spiritual potential. While he taught millions to read, he also taught hundreds of thousands, if not millions, how to pray or how to pray more effectively. His little booklets on prayer along with his own personal teaching and lecturing led vast numbers of persons in many parts of the world into a more fulfilling walk with God.

## E. Stanley Jones's Background

Frank Laubach's birth wasn't the only big thing that happened in 1884. The new year was just three days old when E. Stanley Jones was born in Clarksville, Maryland. Clarksville? That sounds as impressive as Benton, Pennsylvania.

As a boy of seventeen, Jones went to Memorial Church to hear a rough-hewn evangelist, Robert J. Bateman. Jones reported later that he said to himself, "I want what he has." For three days young Jones sought, and on the fourth evening he found. "As I rose from my knees," he recalled years later, "I felt I wanted to put my arms around the world and share this with everybody."[2] As it turned out, that's pretty much what E. Stanley Jones did for the rest of his life: he put his arms around the world to love its inhabitants to Christ.

He graduated from little Asbury College, in Wilmore, Kentucky— a far cry from Laubach's experience at Columbia University in New York City. This goes to show what variety God uses in the divine economy. While an Asbury student, Stanley gave a talk on missions. He prayed that God would give him one missionary as a result of his talk. His prayer was answered; he felt a personal call to the mission field. No sermon is better than one that convinces the person who preaches it.

## E. Stanley Jones the Missionary

During his long lifetime, Jones made a particular impact on India, his main missionary commitment, but also on Japan and on the United States. He established a significant friendship with Mahatma Gandhi. Although he never converted Gandhi to Christianity, he made a great impression on Gandhi while also learning from him. Dr. Jones was so respected in international circles that in December, 1941, he became the personal intermediary from the Emperor of Japan to President Franklin Roosevelt. The timing failed, and the attack on Pearl Harbor happened on December 7. However, the emperor later said that if President Roosevelt's cable—sent at Dr. Jones's direction—had come one day earlier, the Pacific war need never have happened.

For all his influence at such strategic levels and for his several best-selling books, E. Stanley Jones had one unceasing theme: "Christ has been, and is, to me the Event. Everything started with him."[3]

## God's Secret Agenda

So 1884 was a very good year. A flood in Lawrenceburg, Indiana, a coal mine disaster in Virginia, and an extraordinarily shoddy presidential campaign took the headlines, while babies were quietly born in Benton, Pennsylvania, and Clarksville, Maryland. God was at work in two rather modest homes, using godly parents to prepare two great world citizens. While the newspapers concentrated on the economy, the political campaign, and disasters small and large, God was doing special things that would make their impact on the world of the twentieth century.

Mind you, the newspapers are not to be blamed for finding their headlines where they did or for missing the story in the Laubach and Jones babies. We can't expect newspaper or television reporters to be quite that prescient. Nevertheless a writer in the book of Psalms had a feeling for it. At least twenty-five centuries ago this poet wrote,

> When the LORD restored the fortunes of Zion,
> we were like those who dream.
> Then our mouth was filled with laughter,
> and our tongue with shouts of joy;
> then it was said among the nations,
> "The LORD has done great things for them." (Ps. 126:1–2)

The poet wrote those words after his nation had passed through a very rough time, a period when they had gone "out weeping" (Ps. 126:6). The situation was bad, and the prospects worse. But in the midst of it all, God was nevertheless at work. The times are never too difficult for God or beyond the reach of God's purposes. The divine restoration was so wondrous that the people thought they must be dreaming! If the people who despaired in 1884 could only have known how God was at work in the world, they might have sung like the ancient psalmist. They might have said, "We may 'sow in tears,' but some day we will 'reap with shouts of joy'" (Ps. 126:5).

At the beginning of 1984, I preached the following words:

Now it is 1984. A continuing uneasiness plagues our world. It has partly to do with our nation's economy. We're told that we're on the upswing; but millions are still unemployed, and the national debt continues to mount. And we're concerned with good reason about what is unfolding on the international scene. We worry about relationships among the so-called great powers. We also wonder if one of the smaller nations, or some vagrant dictator, might someday set off a powder keg of destruction. Such feelings have no particular logic to them, but still something about the very term "1984" is portentous. George Orwell's novel has made it so. Does a fearful, totalitarian world lie not far ahead?

Some three decades later these words still ring true to our situation. No one can predict with any certainty what the future holds, whether the field of concern is politics, economics, social mores, or for that matter, the next baseball season. Nevertheless, I am very sure of this: *God is at work in our world!* God's attention is not limited to the predictably great places and notable people. If anything, both the scriptures and history suggest that God seems to have a prejudice for people and places that are otherwise overlooked.

We watch for headlines from London, New York, Paris, or Singapore, while God is at work in homes where people—including single parents—are trying to raise their children with godly discipline and faith. God is at work in schools where teachers try to do their best and in churches and Sunday schools where clergy and a host of volunteers do their thing week after week.

As it turned out, 1884 was a very good year. The newspapers didn't know it; they didn't know that God was bringing two missionary statesmen into existence. Of course, nobody knows all that God is doing just now. Even those persons who try earnestly to serve God have only a dim idea of what is unfolding in the midst of their daily routine. Be sure of this! All of us who try to practice our Christianity in the daily round of our home, our work, our politics, and our daily influence are involved in God's grand enterprise of goodness.

Who knows if some preacher or teacher, a hundred years from now, will look back on the footnotes of history and say, "1984, or our current year, was a very good year. God was at work, so that instead of disaster, hope and salvation appeared."

*You*, blessed be God, can be part of the grand story.

# CHAPTER 19

# Dorothy Day
## An Impatient Saint

Persons with an uneven spiritual profile hold particular potential for biographical sermons. That's why, when we're preaching biblical biographical sermons, we're drawn to Jacob, David, and Peter. That's part of the appeal of Dorothy Day.

### Introducing Dorothy Day

Born in 1897, Dorothy left her imprint on a good part of the twentieth century. She grew up in a home where religion was vigorously rejected, yet found herself continually drawn to Christ. A restless soul, she rejected religion in her early university days after baptism into the Episcopal Church as a teenager. She left college after only two years to immerse herself in the bohemian lifestyle of Greenwich Village. In that period, legendary literary figures could be found everywhere in the Village. Dorothy became involved with some of the most exciting and controversial of the lot.

But the Hound of Heaven stayed on her trail. Dorothy converted to Catholicism. She was devout and passionate in her faith, but always with a protest in her soul. That restlessness led her to establish (with Peter Maurin) the Catholic worker movement. *Newsweek* magazine called her "the most influential Roman Catholic of her time." That is saying a good deal since her influence began in the 1930s and continued until her death in 1980.

As a political activist, she fought a legion of causes: the needs of the poor, the rights of workers, and strict pacifism. She maintained her pacifist position even during World War II, and in spite of FBI investigations into her conduct and influence. Controversy seemed at times to be her meat and drink. In her own church, Roman Catholicism, she was seen as everything from a radical troublemaker to a walking saint.

### Basic Background

Dorothy May Day was born in Brooklyn, New York, on November 8, 1897, to John and Grace Day. The family moved to California in 1904 and to Chicago some three years later. During these years, Dorothy was confirmed and baptized in the Episcopal Church. She spent two years at the University of Illinois, then moved to New York City, which for much of the rest of her life was her home, or at least her base of operation. On December 28, 1927, she was baptized into the Catholic Church. On May 1, 1933, she and Peter Maurin produced the first edition of *Catholic Worker,* a name that was to define Dorothy and her movement from that time forward. She died November 29, 1980.

### Communities of Interest

Even a quarter of a century after her death, Dorothy Day evokes strong feelings along the political spectrum. People committed to causes of social justice, labor rights, better distribution of wealth, and world peace are always drawn to Dorothy Day. Just as surely, some will always see her as an irresponsible political and economic radical. She is particularly appealing to Catholics and to idealists of every age. People with some knowledge or interest in knowing about the literary scene of the 1920s, the economic scene of the Depression, or the political scene of World War II are readily drawn to this irregular, charismatic personality.

## SERMON _____

# Dorothy Day: *An Impatient Saint*

## Scripture Lesson: Ephesians 6:10–17

Great phrases quickly become meaningless clichés, so I hesitate to speak the term that comes to my mind. But I must. Dorothy Day was a legend in her own time. The term is used these days to describe people with only the requisite fifteen minutes of fame, but Dorothy

May Day deserved the title. She showed her potential while still in her early twenties. In her most secular and amoral period, she became part of the literary community of Greenwich Village during the headiest days of that fabled neighborhood. Then, not long after her conversion, she became a polarizing personality in the Catholic Church in America. The Catholic worker movement she founded with Peter Maurin was symbolic of the spiritual and economic ferment of an entire generation. If any individual can be seen as the icon of the church's attempt to confront human need at its most dramatic levels, Dorothy Day is that person.

## Dorothy Day's Background

Dorothy Day was an unlikely prospect for such a calling. Let me tell you her story. She was born into a home where she was taught "Now I lay me down to sleep," but little more in the way of religion. Her father, John, professed to be an atheist, although Dorothy remembers that he always had a Bible in reach. Her mother, Grace, sought primarily to please her husband, so the children were not baptized. John was a newspaperman, and Dorothy apparently inherited those genes. She eventually established one of the most controversial newspapers of her time.

When Dorothy was seven years old, her father moved the family from Brooklyn, where all four of the children had been born, to California. There Dorothy had her first memorable religious experience. On a rainy Sunday afternoon, she stumbled upon a Bible in the attic of their California home and read it for several hours. Only seven at the time, she had been reading for three years. Something about the book captivated her. Years later, she said she had a sense that day that she was "handling something holy." At age eight, she went several times to a Methodist church with a neighbor family. She loved the hymns, but she found that her experiences in the church were not something to be talked about at home.

After three years in California, John Day moved his family to Chicago despite having no job. Eventually he became sports editor of a Chicago newspaper. In Chicago, Dorothy experienced the Episcopal Church. She is often described as being "haunted" by God. The phrase makes sense when one reads her story.

In a home where God was rather purposely shut out, Dorothy found God constantly seeking admission. She loved the psalms and the prayers in the Episcopal Church, just as she had loved the hymns in the Methodist Church. In time she was baptized and confirmed in the Episcopal Church, though afterward she had little memory of the experience. She read the sermons of John Wesley, the lives of the early saints, and *The Imitation of Christ.* One marvels at this hunger, since the girl had no setting in which to nurture it.

## Self-assertive Years

Even the most earnest spiritual hunger needs some kind of structured sustenance. At sixteen, as a freshman at the University of Illinois, she immersed herself in ideas she found exciting, especially as those ideas gave her a sense of rebellious freedom. She began to swear, especially around those who would be shocked by her swearing. She found something self-asserting about lighting up a cigarette as she stepped out of a classroom. Not surprisingly, she decided that she was an atheist. This gave her another instrument for shocking people.

Classes often bored Dorothy. Later in life, she said the only benefit she got from her two years at the University was her friendship with Rayna Simons and her own sense of complete independence. Rayna Simons, a Jewish girl from a wealthy family, became Dorothy's closest friend during this period. She provided a good many advantages that Dorothy wouldn't otherwise have been able to enjoy. Through this friendship Dorothy moved into the world of ideas and of vigorous intellectual discussion in a measure she hadn't previously known. The only part God played in Dorothy's life at this time was as a topic of discussion that reduced God to a test tube issue. Dorothy did not experience the kind of reality that would later make ultimate claims on her life.

## Dorothy Day in New York

In the summer following her sophomore year at the University, Dorothy moved with her family back to New York City. There, entirely against her father's wishes, she sought work with a newspaper. Her father, a lifelong newspaperman, felt a newspaper office was no place for a woman. Dorothy insisted that his interference prevented her getting a job. At last she found work with *Call,* a socialist paper. Dorothy had embraced socialism at the University, so the job was compatible with her convictions—convictions that at the time were highly theoretical with little sense of how they might be worked out in the real world.

New York proved to be an exciting world for a girl as young as Dorothy. In this world all the standard moral and political verities were scorned. As a demonstrator for woman's suffrage, she was arrested and put in jail, but not before she left her teeth marks on the officer who handcuffed her. As a resident of Greenwich Village, she enjoyed the friendship of Malcolm Cowley, Max Bodenheim, and Eugene O'Neill–again, an exciting world for a young woman who wanted to write. Some say Dorothy was the inspiration for one of the characters in O'Neill's play, *Moon for the Misbegotten*. Whether true or not, there's no question of the intense friendship they enjoyed for a time.

## Dorothy Day's Personal Relationships

Then Lionel Moise came into her life. Dorothy hesitated over the years about letting her biography be written because she felt that a biographer might make too much of her moral failures and that young people might use her conduct as an excuse for similar conduct. Eventually, she became pregnant by Moise, and at his insistence she endured an abortion. As a person who later fully supported the Catholic opposition to abortion, this part of her life remained a burden of regret.

After breaking up with Moise, Dorothy was married briefly to Barkeley Tobey, another resident of the literary world who during his lifetime had eight marriages. Dorothy felt she had only used Tobey in rebounding from her relationship with Moise. Then came a common law marriage to a biologist by training and an anarchist by conviction, out of which came Dorothy's only child, her daughter Tamar.

If you're a bit of a Bible student, you may wonder why Dorothy named her daughter Tamar. I do. Perhaps it was by chance. In any event, it adds to the romance of Dorothy's spiritual pilgrimage. Tamar was the dark heroine, if I may call her that, of a strange story in the thirty-eighth chapter of Genesis. Her name carries through into the New Testament because she is one of the four women mentioned in the genealogy of our Lord. In a sense, she is the essence of redemption: a human caught in hopeless circumstances who follows a shameful course but is a crucial actor in God's unfolding plan. A little like Dorothy Day. But of course, I'm putting interpretations into Dorothy's story; that's the preacher in me. I can't help finding messages of hope and redemption in unlikely corners.

## Doing Business with God

One thing is certain: the birth of Tamar forced Dorothy to do business with the God who had so unceasingly pursued her. Again and again along the way, in her years of declared atheism or religious scorn, Dorothy had moved tentatively toward God. She read a Bible during her jail time. Repeatedly, she sought out churches where she could stop to pray. What she was doing was contrary to what she was saying and to the life style of her circle of friends. As is true with many of us, Dorothy wanted for her child what she had never fully appropriated for herself. Dorothy was twenty-eight when Tamar was born. Her life to that point had followed an extremely erratic course. However, now she felt one thing was certain: Tamar must be baptized!

So Tamar was baptized, but with the baptism, Forster left. Dorothy realized the inevitability of it. Forster insisted that as an anarchist and an atheist he could never agree to a wedding ceremony before officials of either church or state. Dorothy had already decided, before Tamar was baptized, that she herself would become Catholic. She struggled through all the obstacles in her way, but knew it must be. On a gray, foggy December 28, 1927, with "no sense of peace, no joy, no conviction that what I was doing was right," she was baptized and became part of the church. Later, as she looked back on her long and erratic soul-journey, she realized that all through the years "it was God who had been the object of her passionate seeking."[1]

## Dorothy Day and The Catholic Worker Movement

Once Dorothy's heart was fixed on its ultimate destination, she set her life on full speed ahead. Both the direction and the speed got new impetus when Peter Maurin moved into her life. He had heard that she needed a Catholic education, and he intended to give it to her. Dorothy ever after saw his coming as an act of Providence. Maurin, a Frenchman by birth and a philosopher by nature, liked nothing better than to share his "ideas" with anyone who would listen. Indeed, the only way people could avoid listening was to leave him, because he was an inveterate talker. Dorothy mirrored his ideas and his passion for justice and the poor, and so she teamed up with him to establish the Catholic worker movement.

The principles of the Catholic worker movement were simple, so simple they frightened people. The movement wanted to change the social order, to help its victims. They intended to do so in the name and spirit of Christ in the belief that to follow Christ is to love one's neighbor and that loving one's neighbor is a matter of deeds as well as words. They began with the barest of facilities on New York City's lower East Side, offering food and shelter.

In time, worker houses appeared in Canada, England, Australia, and Mexico, as well as in more than thirty locations in the United States. Maurin's vision was that those who came for help would also work to maintain the houses. He wanted them to become "scholars" in their understanding of the practical ministry of the church. In Maurin's mind, workers must be scholars, and scholars must be workers.

From the start the worker movement emphasized the inherent dignity of each person. Those who aligned themselves with the movement practiced voluntary poverty. Several times Miss Day established small farms in the hope that many of the derelicts who came their way might find a new life in the setting of farm labor.

## Dorothy Day and the *Catholic Worker*

Because the houses and the farms operated as communes, critics often branded the Catholic worker movement as Communist. This was an easy title to give during a long period of the twentieth century when the Communist scare abroad made for Communist fears at home. Those who saw this threat in the movement and in Dorothy herself found ample ammunition once she and Peter Maurin began publishing the *Catholic Worker.* The fact that they seemed simply to revise the name of the best-known Communist publication made it easy for their critics to see an association. The first issue of the *Catholic Worker* appeared on May 1, 1933. One could buy it on the streets for a penny a copy or take it for free when a penny wasn't forthcoming. The most vigorous Catholic voices of the generation wrote for the *Worker.* It was unrelenting in its support of the poor. Its economics often bordered on socialism. It represented the first strong, Catholic, pacifist voice in America and probably did more than any other single force to establish pacifism within American Catholicism.

## Dorothy Day's Faith

Dorothy Day had staked out radical social and economic positions even as a teenager. She often aligned herself with persons and organizations that were at best secular and at worst anti-religious. Still, she remained unbendingly Christian. She believed in "the little way" of Saint Therese, faithfulness in bringing the love of God into the routine affairs of daily life. She said,

> The problem is gigantic. Throughout the world there is homelessness, famine, fear, and war and the threat of war. We live in a time of gigantic evil. It is hopeless to think of combating it by any other means than that of sanctity. To think of overcoming such evil by material means, by alleviations, by changes in the social order only—all this is utterly hopeless.[2]

Knowingly or not, Dorothy Day was echoing Paul, who insisted, "For our struggle is not against enemies of blood and flesh, but against the rulers, against the authorities, against the cosmic powers of this present darkness, against the spiritual forces of evil in the heavenly places" (Eph. 6:12). Like Paul, she would put on an armor daily; and, like him, she would perform no act of violence, nothing, that is, except the incessant storming of the principles and strongholds of evil.

The fight was never easy. Leaders in the church she loved often attacked her. Still, she remained utterly faithful to the church. Her supporters often fled, sometimes because she was so unswerving that she insisted on alienating them. Some people she trusted betrayed her. Some of her most enthusiastic ideas ended in embarrassing failure. Saint Paul said that "we have this treasure in clay jars, so that it may be made clear that this extraordinary power belongs to God and does not come from us" (2 Cor. 4:7). Dorothy Day knew as much. In one of those moments when she realized the extent of her responsibilities and influence, she wrote in her Journal, "I am a weak and faulty vessel to be freighted with so valuable a message as cargo."[3]

This is a word for every follower of Jesus Christ. We might be more inclined to speak it if, like Dorothy Day, we came more clearly to see the monstrous power of evil and the compassionate love of the Lord Christ.

CHAPTER 20

# Mother Teresa
*God's Little Pencil*

## Introducing Sister Teresa

If popular vote determined the canonization of saints in the Catholic Church, Sister Teresa of Calcutta would have been named a saint in her own lifetime. Indeed, many thousands of people did just that. Anytime she appeared in television or print, someone was likely to comment, "She's a saint. The real article." This evaluation came as easily from Protestants as from Catholics, and even from those who claimed no religious identification.

Now let it be understood that many disliked her, some of them rather emphatically. In almost every instance her opponents resented some of her convictions and feared the impact that might come from her declaring of her convictions. Yet the quality of her life usually impressed even her most vocal critics.

Most of us agree that our times are badly in need of truly worthy heroes. The adulation our generation gives to athletes, entertainers, and a disparate collection of public personalities testifies to our hunger for someone to look up to and perhaps to emulate. We preachers sometimes rail against this misdirected hero worship. We would do better to offer some persuasive alternatives. Mother Teresa offers such a possibility.

### Basic Background

Agnes Gonxha Bojaxhiu was born August 27, 1910, to an Albanian peasant family in Skopje, Yugoslavia. While in school, she became a member of the Sodality of the Sisters of Mary. With several other members of her group she volunteered for the Bengal Mission. In November, 1928, the mission sent her to the Loreto Abbey in Ireland for training and then to India to begin her novitiate in Darjeeling. For some nineteen years she taught geography at St. Mary's High School in Calcutta. For a time she served as principal of the school.

On September 10, her "day of decision," she sought permission from her Superior to live alone outside the cloister, so she could minister in the city's slums. In time, Rome approved her request. On August 8, 1948, she replaced her Loreto habit with a white sari with blue border and a cross on the shoulder, a garb that would become known around the world. After a short, intensive training in nursing, she returned to Calcutta. In December of 1948, she got permission to open her first slum school. In October, 1950, the work of the Missionaries of Charity was approved and set up in Calcutta. From there it spread through India, then steadily around the world: Venezuela, Ceylon, Tanzania, Rome, Australia, Jordan, Europe, and the Americas. She received the Nobel Peace Prize on December 10, 1979, and died September 5, 1997. On October 19, 2003, Pope John Paul II beatified her, bringing her within one step of full canonization as a saint of the Catholic Church.

### Communities of Interest

The generation that watched Mother Teresa become a legendary figure is, of course, interested in her. She also appeals to a younger generation that has come to know her in the latter years of her life or since her death. Few if any persons have such wide recognition and so positive acceptance. Remember, however, we humans have a quality that seems to want to bring down whatever or whoever is widely praised. In some people this quality is particularly virulent. If you tell Mother Teresa's story, you should expect someone (and perhaps several) to speak a negative word. They've heard more of goodness than they want to hear.

---

**SERMON** _____

# Mother Teresa: *God's Little Pencil*

## Scripture Lesson: Matthew 25:31–40

The Catholic Church is very circumspect in declaring someone a saint. Not many years ago it removed the title from many who had been popularly identified as saints because study made the person's identity or achievements uncertain. The process of canonization is lengthy and set with many intentional obstacles. However, the church authorities are speeding up the process in the case of one person—Mother Teresa of Calcutta. A cynic might say that the Catholic Church is wise to do this because Mother Teresa is the church's best public relations symbol since Francis of Assisi.

## Mother Teresa and Francis of Assisi

The cynic would be right at least in one point: that is in comparing the universal appeal of Teresa and Francis. They have in common a wonderful simplicity of faith. Francis could preach to the birds, and Teresa frustrated those who wanted her to use corporate wisdom. Both learned to see Christ in the poorest and most abject souls. Although both are quoted freely and widely, both felt their ministry was in service rather than in words. As Saint Francis said, "It is no use walking anywhere to preach unless we preach as we walk." But their origins were very different.

Francis was the son of a prosperous merchant, raised to a life of comfort. In his early years he engaged in somewhat prodigal ways. After a period in an enemy prison and experiences of poor health, he saw a vision of Christ and changed his way of life. He rejected the family fortune and adopted the way of absolute poverty.

Teresa, on the other hand, was born into an Albanian peasant family in Skopje, Yugoslavia. Malcolm Muggeridge, the British television personality whose conversion to Christ came largely through his experience with Mother Teresa, has said that without God's special grace her peasant background might have made her "a rather hard, and even grasping, person. God has turned these qualities to his own ends."[1]

## Mother Teresa's Background

Teresa's home was simple, but exceptionally happy. When as a school girl she felt called to holy service, she made a great sacrifice to leave the security of love she enjoyed with her parents and siblings. She first felt her call at age twelve. At the time, she had never seen a nun. At eighteen, she went to Ireland to train for missionary service in India. For nineteen years she found her place of service at St. Mary's High School in Calcutta, first as a geography teacher and then as principal of the school. Like many nuns, she showed a real gift for administration. Her ministry was effective and fruitful.

But on September 10, 1947, Teresa received what she ever afterward referred to as the call within a call. Called already to be a nun, now she felt called to go into the poorest streets of Calcutta. She loved her life in the pleasant garden of the Loreto convent with enjoyable colleagues and lively students, but she felt she must take on a more demanding calling. Administrative details consumed two years before she could begin her new work. With those matters completed, Mother Teresa went to the worst part of Calcutta, rented lodging, and began her ministry of love.

## Mother Teresa's Ministry of Love

This ministry of love has endeared her to the poor and to those who believe in the power of love, but sometimes, it has angered those who feel she might better have worked at the political and economic solutions to poverty. The misunderstandings did not seem to bother her. Dominic Lapierre, author and philanthropist, recalls the first time he met Teresa. She was tending to "a living skeleton," speaking to him gently as she cleaned his wounds. When Lapierre introduced himself, Mother Teresa asked a young volunteer to take care of the dying man while she talked with Lapierre. Her instructions to the volunteer were simple, yet almost fierce. "Love him," she said. "Love him with all your strength."[2]

Mother Teresa's philosophy was very simple, indeed, as simple as the commands of Jesus that she took so seriously. When I read about Mother Teresa, I realize again that, with all my years of professed discipleship, I still haven't followed Jesus Christ as he commanded. "I have no imagination," she said. "I cannot imagine God the Father. All I can see is Jesus." But she saw Jesus best in the poor, in whom she saw our Lord "in distressing disguise."[3] This vision was so real to her that whenever she wrote of the poor, she wrote "Poorest of the Poor" in capitals as she did her references to God and to Christ.

On her entrance into the holy life, she had taken the name Teresa after Saint Therese of Lisieux, the "Little Flower." Saint Therese of Lisieux lived a bare twenty-four years but became revered for her faithfulness in small things. When she was proposed for sainthood, someone asked the Pope what she had done. The Pope replied with a single sentence: "I will canonize her because she did ordinary things with extraordinary love."

## Mother Teresa Doing Little Things with Love

This was Mother Teresa's intention from the beginning of her work, even as a very young nun. She meant to do little things, but to do them with love. To her credit she never really veered from this course. It's very difficult to continue being a servant to all when so many tell you that you're the one giving orders. She did, indeed, give orders. She ruled her Missionaries of Charity with a firm and unrelenting hand. But she mopped floors, tended babies, and treated sores along side of the members of her order. As her biographer said, she was "not only humble and small but also strong-willed, resolute, determined and totally fearless, because God was on her side."[4]

I think most people who have accomplished great things for the cause of Christ have possessed the feeling that God was on their side— or perhaps that they were on God's side. This is a source of emotional and spiritual strength, but it can also encourage the abuse of power. I suspect that one restraining factor for Mother Teresa was her complete belief in the Catholic Church and in the office of the Pope. People in general have said, "What Mother wants, she gets." But she brought herself under the discipline of the Church at all times.

## The Growth of Mother Teresa's Work

Mother Teresa's work began to grow in astonishing ways. While most Orders were losing numbers, the Missionaries of Charity grew. The rules were severe, the work strenuous, and the monetary rewards non-existent. Still women were drawn to the task. What had begun as a project for the poor in Calcutta spread, as soon as the structures of the Catholic Church would allow, to other cities in India and then to other parts of the world. But men, too, felt called to the high demands, so in 1963 a Congregation of Brothers was established. Their work, too, aimed to be with "the poorest of the poor in slums, on the streets, and wherever they are found." They would work especially with leprosy patients and with abandoned, homeless boys.

In ways hard to explain, Mother Teresa began to be an international figure. Her picture appeared in newspapers around the world—with Queen Elizabeth II, President and Mrs. Ronald Reagan, Mrs. Indira Gandhi, Yasser Arafat, and Diana, Princess of Wales. Mother Teresa moved as comfortably with the carriers of power as with the wretched of the street. She saw one and all as humans in need of God's love. Although the need might be more obvious in some instances than others, in her mind it was equally real. I am confident that she was theologically correct in this: a human soul is a human soul, equally needy whether king or derelict, and equally valuable in God's sight.

Mother Teresa gave each one the same kind of intense attention. Her biographer, Kathryn Spink, writes of "her gift for giving her whole attention to the person she encountered."[5] Perhaps the degree to which people felt her attention was a gift, but the giving of one's "whole attention" is surely a quality open to any of us willing to be so involved with others. The only secret, I suspect, is a readiness to divest ourselves of our own interests to a degree that we can become thoroughly absorbed in the concerns of another.

## The Little Pencil in God's Hand

With it all, Mother Teresa continued to have an interesting figure of speech to describe herself. She saw herself always as "a little pencil" in God's hand. She believed that God wanted to write a love letter to the world through works of love, and she wanted simply to be the "little pencil" with which God might write.

When I set out on the story of Mother Teresa, I titled it tentatively, "Everybody's Saint." As I did my research, however, I discovered that–of course!–she was not everybody's saint. She offended all sorts of persons, particularly as her work and her reputation grew. Some were critical of her method: they wanted her to work at eliminating the "root causes" of poverty and sickness rather than simply tending to the sick. She tried simply to define her unique role: "We all have a duty to serve God where we feel called," she said. "I feel called to help individuals, not to interest myself in structures or institutions. I do not feel like judging or condemning."[6] Some turned to the old analogy; instead of giving the poor a fish that would feed them for a day, she should teach them how to fish so they could care for themselves in the future. Teresa replied quietly that most of the people served by her order didn't have the strength to hold a fishing pole.

Intellectuals and professional social workers were often critical. She reduced issues to such simple, singular human terms, cutting away all the professional verbiage that she offended many. Feminists were unhappy with her vigorous condemnation of abortion and with her opposition to the ordination of women. Germaine Greer saw her as a religious imperialist.

Some in Calcutta, the city in which her work began and which she considered home (she became an Indian citizen in 1948) felt that the publicity given to her work advertised the city's poverty to the detriment of the city's many cultural values. Still others criticized her willingness to work in countries with repressive regimes, especially when her picture was taken with dictators and tyrants. She responded simply that she would go wherever there was need. "If there are poor on the moon," she said on one occasion, "we shall go there too."[7]

In February, 1994, Mother Teresa came somewhat unwillingly to address the National Prayer Breakfast in Washington, D.C. Much of her rather lengthy speech attacked abortion. There was much applause at its conclusion, but no one at the head table, including

President Clinton, joined in the applause. President Clinton later apologized to her, however, and Hillary Rodham Clinton found common cause with her in the matter of adoption.

Without a doubt, one might find reasons to raise questions about some of her methods, some elements of her theology, and particulars of her work. Personally, however, I remain silent. To paraphrase a term I've heard in another context, I like the way Mother Teresa got the job done better than the way the rest of us don't get it done. I ponder again the words of our Lord: "Woe to you when all speak well of you, for that is what their ancestors did to the false prophets" (Lk. 6:26). You can't be a person of convictions without alienating somebody. And there's no question that Mother Teresa was a person of convictions! Nor was she careful to hide or disguise them.

## Mother Teresa's Legacy

Mother Teresa's body gave out on September 5, 1997, within the same week as the accidental death of Diana, Princess of Wales–a calendar coincidence that gave much lineage to newspaper and pop magazine writers. This was not entirely without reason, because the two women had established something of a friendship. At the time of Mother Teresa's death, there were some 4,000 Sisters in the Missionaries of Charity, over four hundred Brothers, and a host of affiliated persons: Missionary of Charity Fathers, Lay Missionaries of Charity, Co-Workers, and so on. The list of Foundations (various houses of mercy and service) covers nearly nine full pages in the Spink biography, with locations on five continents and many islands of the sea.

But of course the reach goes farther. When Fary Moini, a member of the Rotary Club of La Jolla Golden Triangle, California, received the National Hometown Hero award for her aid to Afghan refugees, she said, "Mother Teresa said we all cannot do great things, but we can do small things with love."[8] When Charles Colson was asked to visit a woman in an isolation cell dying of AIDS, he confessed that he was at first reluctant. "Yet, just the night before, I had seen a television report of Mother Teresa embracing two men with AIDS. If that frail, 90–pound nun could do it, how could I, the strapping ex-Marine, do less?"[9] Without a doubt, several of us have prodded ourselves at one time or another with some similar admonition from Mother Teresa. We invoke her name–particularly because she was part of our century–to stir ourselves to be more of what we think God and life would expect us to be. And why not?

Malcolm Muggeridge said that "something of God's universal love" had rubbed off on Mother Teresa, "giving her homely features a noticeable luminosity; a shining quality."[10] Might something more of God rub off on us? Might we, too, become a pencil in God's hand? Indeed we can, if we are willing to do ordinary things with extraordinary love.

# Notes

## Introduction

[1]Kathleen Norris, *Dakota: A Spiritual Geography* (Boston: Houghton Mifflin Company, 1993), 72.

[2]Hermann Gunkel, "What Remains of the Old Testament" (1914), 52–53; quoted in *A Treasury of Jewish Quotations,* ed. Joseph L. Baron (South Brunswick: A. S. Barnes, 1965), 352.

[3]From Henry Wadsworth Longfellow, "A Psalm of Life."

[4]W. Jackson Bate, *Samuel Johnson* (New York: Harcourt Brace Jovanovich, 1977), xix.

## Chapter 1: Teresa of Avila

[1]Phyllis McGinley, *Saint-Watching* (New York: The Viking Press, 1969), 65.

[2]Cathleen Medwick, *Teresa of Avila: The Progress of a Soul* (New York: Alfred A. Knopf, 1999), 32.

[3]Letter to María de Mendoza, quoted in ibid., 167–68.

[4]Ibid., 145.

[5]Dag Hammarskjold, *Markings* (New York: Alfred A. Knopf, 1964), xxi.

[6]Quoted in McGinley, *Saint-Watching,* 93.

[7]Ibid.

[8]Ibid., 118.

[9]Ibid., 7.

## Chapter 2: John Robinson

[1]George F. Willison, *Saints and Strangers* (New York: Reynal & Hitchcock, 1945), 50.

[2]Robert Merrill Bartlett, *The Pilgrim Way* (Philadelphia: Pilgrim Press, 1971), 221.

[3]Ibid., 221–22.

[4]Willison, *Saints and Strangers,* 481.

## Chapter 3: The King James Bible

[1]David Daniell, *Tyndale's New Testament* (New Haven, Conn.: Yale University Press, 1989), viii..

[2]Ibid., xxvii.

[3]H. S. Miller, *General Biblical Introduction* (Houghton, N.Y.: The Word-Bearer Press, 1940), 338–39.

[4]Gustavus S. Paine, *The Learned Men* (New York: Thomas Y. Crowell Company, 1959), 26.

[5]Ibid., 170.

## Chapter 4: Anne Bradstreet

[1]Anne Bradstreet, *The Works of Anne Bradstreet,* ed. John Harvard Ellis (Charleston: A. E. Cutter, 1867), xiv.

[2]Ibid., 22.

[3]Ibid., 394.

[4]Ibid., 394.

[5]In Roger Lundin and Mark A. Noll, eds., *Voices from the Heart* (Grand Rapids, Mich.: Wm. B. Eerdmans, 1987), 55–58

## Chapter 5: Blaise Pascal

[1]T. S. Eliot, "Introduction," in Blaise Pascal, *Pascal's Pensées* (New York: E. P. Dutton & Co., 1958), x.

[2]Phrase associated with German theologian Friedrich Schleiermacher.

[3]The Pascal quotes in the following section are from Marvin R. O'Connell, *Blaise Pascal: Reasons of the Heart* (Grand Rapids, Mich.: Wm. B. Eerdmans, 1997), 95–96.

[4]Pascal, *Pensées,* section 6, 347.

[5]Ibid., section 3, 233.

[6]Ibid., xvii.

[7]O'Connell, *Blaise Pascal,* 105.

[8]Hugh T. Kerr and John M. Mulder, eds., *Conversions: The Christian Experience* (Grand Rapids, Mich.: Wm. B. Eerdmans, 1983), 38.

## Chapter 6: Johann Sebastian Bach

[1]Richard Dinwiddie, "J. S. Bach: God's Master Musician," *Christianity Today* 29, no. 5 (15 March 1985): 16.

[2]Paul Westermeyer, "Grace and the Music of Bach," *Christian Century* 102, no. 10 (March 20–27, 1985): 292.

[3]Alan Rich, with Katrine Ames, "All Hail Mighty Bach," *Newsweek* 104, no. 27 (24 December 1984): 54–60.

[4]William Buckley, Jr., "Happy Birthday, JSB," *National Review* (3 May 1985): 63.

[5]Elizabeth Knowles, ed., *The Oxford Dictionary of Quotations,* 5th ed. (New York: Oxford Univ. Press, 1999), 326.

[6]Buckley, "Happy Birthday," 63.

[7]Dinwiddie, "Master Musician," 21.

[8]Leonard Bernstein, *Joy of Music* (New York: Simon and Schuster, 1959), 264–65.

[9]Philip Spitta, *Johann Sebastian Bach,* tr. Clara Bell and J. A. Fuller Maitland, vol. 3 (New York: Novello, Ewer & Co., 1889), 318.

## Chapter 7: Ancestors We'd Rather Forget

[1]*Dictionary of Christianity in America: A Comprehensive Resource on the Religious Impulse That Shaped a Continent,* ed. Daniel G. Reid, Robert D. Linder, Harry S. Stout, Bruce L. Shelley (Downer's Grove, Ill.: InterVarsity Press, 1990), 1041.

[2]Ibid.

[3]Arthur Miller, "The Crucible," in *The Contemporary Theatre: The Significant Playwrights of Our Time,* ed. Allan Lewis (New York: Crown, 1988), 9.

[4]Perry Miller, *The New England Mind: From Colony to Province* (Boston: Beacon Press, 1953; Beacon Paperback, 1961), 195.

[5]Robert A. Booth, Jr., "Vita: Samuel Parris," *Harvard Magazine* 94, no. 4 (March-April, 1992): 46.

[6]Ibid., 46.

## Chapter 8: Samuel Johnson

[1]The most recent edition of Boswell's classic biography was published in 1992 by Alfred A. Knopf. Selections from Samuel Johnson's *Dictionary of the English Language* are published from time to time; the full dictionary currently is out of print.

[2]Peter Quennell, *Samuel Johnson, His Friends and Enemies* (New York: American Heritage Press, 1972), 43.

[3]In Elton Trueblood, *Doctor Johnson's Prayers* (Dublin, Ind.: Prinit Press, 1947; paperback edition, 1981), xiii.

[4]Ibid., xi.

[5]Quennell, *Samuel Johnson,* 65–66.

[6]Ibid., 66.

[7]Trueblood, *Doctor Johnson's Prayers,* 1.

[8]Ibid., 7.
[9]Quennell, *Samuel Johnson,* 261.
[10]Ibid., 76.
[11]Ibid., 77.
[12]Trueblood, *Doctor Johnson's Prayers,* xxvii.
[13]David Lyle Jeffrey, ed., *A Burning and a Shining Light* (Grand Rapids, Mich.: Wm. B. Eerdmans, 1987), 322–24.
[14]Walter Jackson Bate, *The Achievement of Samuel Johnson* (New York: Oxford Univ. Press, 1955; Galaxy Book, 1961), 42.

## Chapter 9: John Newton

[1]Steve Turner, *Amazing Grace: The Story of America's Most Beloved Song* (New York: HarperCollins, 2002), 24, 25.
[2]Ibid., 30.
[3]Ibid., 47.

## Chapter 10: A Novel, a Novelist, and a Prophet

[1]From Nathaniel Hawthorne's *American Notebooks,* quoted in Walter Blair, Theodore Hornberger, and Randall Stewart, *The Literature of the United States,* vol. 1 (Chicago: Scott Foresman and Company, 1946), 1065.
[2]D. Bruce Lockerbie, *Dismissing God* (Grand Rapids, Mich.: Baker Books, 1998), 82, 83.
[3]Ibid., 81.
[4]Herman Melville, *Moby-Dick* (New York: Penguin Books, 2003), 197, 198, 200.
[5]Ibid., 44–45.
[6]Ibid., 465.

## Chapter 11: Frederick Douglass

[1]Herman Melville, *Moby-Dick* (New York: Penguin Books, 2003), 45.
[2]Arna Bontemps, *Free at Last: The Life of Frederick Douglass* (New York: Dodd, Mead & Company, 1971), 40.
[3]Edwin S. Gaustad, ed., *Memoirs of the Spirit* (Grand Rapids, Mich.: Wm. B. Eerdmans, 1999), 100.
[4]Bontemps, *Free at Last,* 14.
[5]Ibid., 45.
[6]Gaustad, *Memoirs,* 101, 103.
[7]Ibid., 101.

## Chapter 12: Susan B. Anthony

[1]Mary D. Pellauer, *Toward a Tradition of Feminist Theology* (Brooklyn, New York: Carlson, 1991), 153.
[2]Ibid., 165.
[3]Ibid., 161.
[4]Ibid., 175.
[5]Ibid., 170.
[6]Ibid., 199.

## Chapter 13: Fanny J. Crosby

[1]Andrew Fletcher, "An Account of a Conversation," as quoted in *The Interpreter's Bible,* vol. 4 (New York: Abingdon Press, 1955), 519.
[2]Fanny Crosby, "Rescue the Perishing," *The United Methodist Hymnal* (Nashville: The United Methodist Publishing House, 1989), no. 591.
[3]Bernard Ruffin, *Fanny Crosby* (Philadelphia: United Church Press, 1976), 231.

## Chapter 14: Emily Dickinson

[1]Quoted in the Internet Daily Report from *The Chronicle of Higher Education,* citing an item from *Oxford American* (January/February 2003).
[2]From Roger Lundin, *Emily Dickinson and the Art of Belief* (Grand Rapids, Mich.: Wm. B. Eerdmans, 1998), 48.
[3]Ibid., 49.
[4]Ibid., 43.
[5]Ibid., 52.
[6]Emily Dickinson, *The Complete Poems of Emily Dickinson,* ed. Thomas H. Johnson (Boston: Little, Brown and Company, nd), v.
[7]*Dictionary of American Writers* (Springfield, Mass.: Merriam-Webster, 2001), 112.
[8]Lundin, *Art of Belief,* 3, 5.
[9]Ibid., 84.
[10]*The Complete Poems of Emily Dickinson,* #1551.
[11]Ibid., #1380.
[12]Ibid., #1433.
[13]Ibid., #712.
[14]Ibid., #1052.

## Chapter 15: Frances Willard

[1]Ruth Bordin, *Frances Willard* (Chapel Hill, N.C.: The University of North Carolina Press, 1986), 4.
[2]Ibid., 29.
[3]Ibid., 97.
[4]Ibid., 210.

## Chapter 17: George Washington Carver

[1]Rackham Holt, *George Washington Carver, An American Biography* (Garden City, N. Y.: Doubleday, Doran and Company, 1943), 27.
[2]Basil Miller, *George Washington Carver* (Grand Rapids, Mich.: Zondervan Publishing House, 1943), 43.
[3]Ibid., 56.
[4]Ibid., 34.
[5]Holt, *American Biography,* 255.
[6]Ibid., 247.
[7]Ibid., 314.
[8]Miller, *George Washington Carver,* 118–19.
[9]Ibid., 143, 165.

## Chapter 18: It Was a Very Good Year

[1]Frank Laubach, *The World Is Learning Compassion* (Westwood, N.J.: F. H. Revell Co., 1958), 11.
[2]E. Stanley Jones, *A Song of Ascents* (Nashville: Abingdon Press, 1968), 28.
[3]Ibid., 16.

## Chapter 19: Dorothy Day

[1]William D. Miller, *Dorothy Day: A Biography* (San Francisco: Harper & Row, 1982), 197.
[2]Ibid., 431.
[3]Ibid., 309.

## Chapter 20: Mother Teresa

[1]Malcolm Muggeridge, *Something Beautiful for God* (London: Collins, 1971), 18.
[2]"Mother Teresa is still offering a hand at 84," *The Plain Dealer,* 19 December 94, 11–B.
[3]Kathryn Spink, *Mother Teresa* (San Francisco: Harper SanFrancisco, 1997), 70.
[4]Ibid., vii.
[5]Ibid., vi.
[6]Ibid., 247.
[7]Ibid., 102
[8]"California Rotarian named a 'Hometown Hero,'" *The Rotarian* (August 2003): 8.
[9]"Beyond Condoms," *Christianity Today* 47, no. 6 (June 2003): 64.
[10]Muggeridge, *Something Beautiful,* 17–18.

# Index